The Dream That Saved My Life

by Carolann Bruce

Published by JJMoffs Independent Book Publisher 2020

Author's Note
The events described here are based on my memories and a dairy which was kept by my family throughout my journey. The identifying features of people have been changed in order to protect their privacy and situations have been merged to further protect identities. Any similarities are purely coincidental.

JJMoffs Independent Book Publisher Ltd
Grove House Farm, Grovewood Road,
Misterton, Nottinghamshire DN10 4EF

Cover design by Jeremy Hopes
Typeset by Anna Richards

When you stand and face the sun,
your shadows are always behind you.

Dedications

I dedicate this book to my 'small' but 'mighty' and 'amazing' family.
To my very own angels on earth, Mum, Jed, Jenna, Ryan, Stuart and Kimberley thank you for your support throughout my journey.
And to my two wonderful grandchildren Haydn and Madison who gave me the best hugs and kisses and kept me upbeat.
To my dear brother, Anthony, keep strong we are so proud of you.
To my wonderful son-in-law Darryl thank you for making my daughter so happy.
To Grace Rowland who was sadly taken by COVID.
To Harry Wright a bright star taken too soon and missed by all.
To my dear friends Diane and Kirsty sleep well.

xxxxxxxxxxx

Too Scared to Sleep

Have you ever experienced strange and terrifying dreams? Those that scare you so much you are too afraid to go to sleep? Well that was exactly what had been happening to me over the past year. It was another very late night and I was once again sitting up in bed fighting the urge to sleep; reading, watching TV, anything that would stop me from closing my eyes and falling asleep. My eyelids are so heavy, and I can barely keep my eyes open. I'm yawning, I'm so tired, but I will not go to sleep – not if I can help it. And then … I am gone, unable to fight the tiredness anymore, drifting into the darkness, into the unknown world of dreams once again, into my own strange abyss. The shadows, the strange people, the noises, the images – all trying to warn me of my upcoming fate. But I'm running, fighting the strange things I'm seeing, terrified once again but trapped in my nightmare and desperately trying to wake up, 'WAAAKE UP … WAAAKE UP!' I'm suddenly aware I'm shouting this: 'WAAAKE UP!' and suddenly I am bolt upright in bed, beads of sweat dripping from my forehead, my chest heaving with exhaustion and fear.

Strange and weird but then, this is me.

Peculiar things had been happening to me from as far back as I can remember. I think I was a strange child; no, I *know* I was a strange child! I would often walk alone in the dark through back lanes and alleys instead of sticking to the main roads and I'd have been in so much trouble if my mum had known. My friends would be too scared to join me and would instead stay safely on the main road welcoming the protection from the streetlights, meeting back up with me at the end of my alternative route which eventually took me back to their path. I also used to love wandering through the local cemetery on my own at night. My friends wouldn't come with me and who could blame them? I was fascinated by death and the afterlife and I loved the peace and tranquillity of the cemetery, which always made me feel safe. There – I told you I was weird! My friends would all dare each other to walk through the cemetery alone, and none of them would take up the challenge, except for me. Even though I was afraid of what might be lurking in the dark, I also relished that feeling of been afraid. So yes, I think you could say I was definitely a strange child.

I can also recall knowing when things were going to happen before they actually did. As a child I found that on some occasions I was able to 'predict' things, and this had helped me out of a couple of tricky situations before they actually happened. I wish this had been the case in my adult life, but sadly it's not. I now always listen to my gut feeling, and it has never failed me yet. In fact, it's helped me so much throughout my life.

I am drawn to certain people and I believe that we meet people for a reason. I also think it is important to pay attention to anything you are naturally drawn to; in my experience it often turns out to be something connected to your own path, passion or purpose in life. I believe that our paths are already set in life and although you never know what is around the corner, there are no wrong turnings; everything happens for a reason. My life journey may not always have been plain sailing, but everything I learnt from what happened to me has made me a stronger, more determined and positive person. One of my favourite quotes it this: 'Does the walker choose the path or does the path choose the walker?'

I am not saying I am psychic; I am not – far from it. But I am very aware of the afterlife, ghosts and spirits. Most of my encounters with the spirit world had been during traumatic times in my life, of which, fortunately, I have only experienced a few. Family members would appear very briefly just to let me know they were watching over me. For example, my dear brother, who passed away when he was just five years old, made his first visit to see me when I was in the early stages of labour with my first child. At that point no drugs had entered my body; I was fully conscious and aware. (Thirty-six hours later I was seeing all sorts of strange things but that's quite a different story!) I was alone in my room, lying on my side resting. I had a strange feeling someone was watching me and when I turned to see who had entered my room, there he was: my brother standing at the side of my bed looking at me. He didn't stay for very long though, largely because as soon as I saw him, I screamed in fright and he was gone, as quick as that. I wish I had been braver so I could have studied him more, spent just a few more precious moments with him, but no, I frightened him away with my screams and unfortunately, he has never returned to visit me again. I think he got more of a fright that night than I did!

My son and daughter also both experienced 'sightings' in our previous home. One night, my partner Jed and I were awoken by the sound of screaming, followed by a loud crash. It had come from my son's room. He sounded terrified. We ran to his room to check on him. He was cowering in the corner, his hands covering his eyes, too afraid to even look at us. He always slept with the lamp on as he had experienced many 'sightings' in his room, and he thought that by keeping the light on it would protect him.

He said he had been asleep but then woken up with a strange feeling that someone was watching him. He had opened his eyes to see who was in his room and had nearly had a heart attack when he saw a small, plump woman dressed in a maid's outfit, her hands clasped together in front of her. She was standing right next to his bed, looking at him. He got such a fright that he had jumped up and run down his bed, tripping over the metal bedframe at the end and knocking over a lamp as he went, causing the crash we heard. In my experience, once you scream and make a fuss, the spirit or ghost tends to go away but he said when he looked back to check she'd gone, he got another shock as she was still standing there.

She was still facing his bed, her hands were still clasped, and he watched as she turned her head slowly to look at him. He was absolutely terrified and she only disappeared from sight when we ran into his bedroom.

These type of events happened a lot in our house with both my children experiencing strange sightings. The first night we moved into the house my daughter woke to find a tall man dressed in grey trousers and a suit jacket standing watching her as she slept. She could feel his energy was not good, and was so afraid of him that she couldn't even call out to get our attention. She just lay very still, her eyes tightly closed and cried herself back to sleep. Talk about being frozen stiff.

Later, when researching the history of the house, we discovered it had been the living quarters for the maids and servants who had served at the manor, (which was also on the grounds), and that the manor itself had been haunted by family members who had been murdered in and around the grounds. The information dated back to the 1600s and we began to wonder if we were being 'visited' by their spirits. It certainly appeared so.

★★★

I was brought up on a small island and lived close to the beach. It was a great place to grow up. When I was about seven or eight years old, we moved into a hotel. There were a lot of stairs leading to the different landings where the guest rooms were situated, and on one particular staircase (which led to my bedroom) I had seen, on many occasions, a young boy dressed in very old-fashioned wartime clothes standing on the middle stair. He had a very wobbly leg – I remember thinking it looked like it was only just hanging on – and he always stood on the same staircase, and always on the same stair, holding his wooden crutch. I would only catch quick glimpses of him but each time, I felt just as afraid as if it were the first time. I was too afraid to go past him to get to my bedroom and would run back down the stairs. When I returned only seconds later, he would be gone. I mentioned it at the time to my mum but I don't think she understood what I'd seen and, like most parents, they understandably dismiss some of the strange things their children say.

Many years later, we went back to visit the island so I could show my partner, Jed, where I had grown up. We made a visit to the local museum, where they had a fabulous display all about the island during World War II. There were photos of war camps and there, slap bang in the middle of the photos was our hotel. Only there was barbed wire around the perimeter and soldiers of all ages standing outside on guard. Many hotels at that time were used as hospitals and prisons and the prisoners included artists and teachers, who were deemed 'enemies of the state' because of their nationality. It was fascinating to glean all this information as it confirmed to me that the young boy, I saw on the stairs all those years ago had been a soldier and would have been at the camp recovering. That would explain his leg injury and his wartime clothes. Why his spirit still lingered in the hotel decades later, I have no idea, but it was satisfying to get some affirmation to one of the experiences I'd had as a child. I felt vindicated.

When I was about thirteen years old, I was sitting on

the promenade minding my own business when a teenage girl leaned over the flat roof above and asked what I was doing. She jumped down to join me and we got talking. She told me she lived in a hotel behind where we sat and said she wanted to show me 'something strange'. Nowadays, you would never go off with a stranger, especially after only knowing them for ten minutes, but back then it was quite normal. We lived in a holiday resort and made friends easily with the holidaymakers. Lots of my friends also lived in hotels and you could walk into pretty much any hotel at any time without being questioned. So, I thought nothing of it when she invited me back.

We were in her bedroom and she had a big glass mirror which she had stuck the letters of the alphabet around, as well as the words 'YES', 'NO', 'HELLO' and 'GOODBYE'. She said she could talk to spirits and asked if I wanted to have a go. I was intrigued and agreed. I put my finger gently on the rim of the glass and as soon as she said, 'is anybody there?' the glass slowly began to move to 'YES'.

I said, 'It's you moving it, I'm not stupid'!

But she was adamant she wasn't.

'Ask it any question you want. Something you know I won't know the answer to.'

So, I said out loud,

'What is my gran's name?' and as it spelt out J E A N. I had tears in my eyes and nearly fainted. My gran was called Jean! How the hell was this happening?

From that night on I became obsessed with the Ouija board, using it every day. Sometimes the glass would move so fast across the mirror that we couldn't keep our fingers on it, and as our fingers lost contact with the glass, it would suddenly stop. I can't explain any of this, but the more, strange activity we encountered, the more obsessed we became. We had no idea what we were dealing with.

We had no Internet in our home in the early 1980s, no access to mobile phones and we lived on an island, where we only had local news. The Ouija board became our focus and the following incident baffles me to this day: The board had attracted a young girl who told us she had been murdered. She told us the story of how it had all happened, even giving us the initials of the person who had killed her. The girl had only recently been murdered and her body not yet been found. She had been missing for a couple of weeks. We were keeping notes of all the things we found out but the information we received from this young girl was firmly engraved in my mind and I didn't need notes to remind me of all the details.

I won't go into too much detail for my own personal reasons but twenty years on, I decided to do a Google search to see if there had been any murders which might have been similar to what she told us. I was shocked to the core when the name of the girl we had spoken to popped up. The name of the man who had killed her matched the initials we'd been given, as did the story of her disappearance, including what she had been doing the day she went missing. All the details were exactly the same as she had told us twenty years previously, right down to what she'd been swinging in her hand. Seeing her photo online sent goose pimples down my spine. It had taken over twenty years for her killer to be caught, so how could I have known all that information when it wasn't released for a further twenty years? And how did the glass spell out my gran's name? These are questions that remain unanswered to this day.

The final time I used the Ouija board followed another incident that could not be explained, though I knew from what had happened, that it was time to stop. We had lifted the glass from the mirror as we thought we had a 'bad spirit' in the glass (we were young and inexperienced). Every time we put our fingers on the glass it moved around uncontrollably until our fingers lost contact and the glass fell over. So, I picked the small tumbler up and held it on the palm of my hand. We were laughing at it when I said, 'You're not as strong now, are you? What are you going to do now?'

The glass popped and I was left holding lots of little glass crystals in my hand. It scared me so much that I never used the Ouija board again. There was no explaining this away and my gut feeling was telling me to stop; this was getting dangerous.

My new friend told me all about other 'ghostly' experiences that she had had in her hotel. They had two hotels next door to each other with access through a door on the first-floor landing. During the war these hotels had been used as a hospital. She told me that one side of the hotel was more haunted than the other. Rumour had it, it was more haunted because that part of the hospital had housed the 'sicker' patients; ones likely to die. She claimed there was old lady who wore a caped hood and wandered slowly through the corridors. She had seen the lady many times, she said.

One afternoon we were sitting having a chat when

she said she needed to get a drink. She left me alone and went off to get one. A few minutes later I heard a strange noise, and when I turned around, there she was: the old lady with her cloak over her head, very slowly crossing the corridor between the two hotels, exactly as my friend told me. I screamed so loudly and got such a fright that I fell off the bar stool I was perching on. Scrabbling around on the floor, I looked desperately for somewhere to run to. I was terrified and my heart was hammering in my chest. I got up and started to run, still screaming. As I looked behind me, I saw she had dropped to the floor; her cloak had fallen off, and there, in place of the hooded lady, was my strange new friend laughing uncontrollably on the floor. There was no old lady. She had well and truly tricked me.

As I said, it's usually when I'm having a traumatic time in my life that I see real apparitions, ghosts, or spirits. Luckily, I haven't had too many traumatic times, which is just as well – I don't think I could cope with having too many encounters with those who have passed over to the other side. I don't even like watching ghost films; they terrify me, so to see them up close and real is absolutely terrifying. I am not a specialist in any aspect of the paranormal, and therefore I'm not sure which word best describes what I have seen and experienced. I don't claim to have professional knowledge of this subject; I can only tell you about some of my experiences, which even I cannot fully understand to this day, as a layperson.

I do believe my whole family are receptive and open to these visitors. When my son went to see a spiritualist for a reading, she told him he had the 'gift' and that the spirits were telling her she had to teach him how to use his gift, instead of giving him an actual reading. And when my granddaughter was very young, she was visited by many different spirits. She would relate entire conversations she'd had with them! One spirit told her she was her angel, which was nice, although eventually we had to ask them to stop visiting her: a male figure told her he was a doctor and claimed to be her 'other daddy'. (Doesn't sound great, does it?) It was confusing and frightening for her. When we asked them not to visit anymore, they did as we asked and never returned. As a small child, my mum had similar experiences; she would also get nightly visits from spirits and have full conversations with them. And I have vivid memories of my gran reading the tea leaves from our cups - she would try to teach me how to interpret what we saw. So, we have all been believers as far back as I can remember.

It has been said that the spirits can talk to you in your sleep, put thoughts into your mind and even show you a glimpse into your future. But you have to listen and believe what they are trying to tell you. I am so glad I'm receptive to this activity because, little did I know at the time, all the paranormal activity I experienced as a child, would one day re-emerge within my dreams, allowing me more than a glimpse into my future. This 'glimpse', when it arrived, was more like watching a real life movie, and it gave me a choice. Having this choice and the knowledge of what was to come would eventually save my life. For this I will be forever truly grateful to the spirits.

They are Everywhere

I am a qualified nurse and when I chose this profession it shocked my mum as I was no good with needles or blood! In fact, I went for a job as phlebotomist, (someone who takes blood samples), before training as a nurse, not actually knowing what the role entailed. At the interview the consultant stuck a rather large needle into his leather desk and asked, 'How are you with needles?'

I went so light-headed I wanted to pass out, but I managed to keep control and upright, and a week later I was offered the job. In my new role, I had many occasions when the dreaded faint came over me and if I was in the middle of taking a lot of blood samples from one patient, I would have to stop halfway through, make my apologies and leave the room. I would then return and re-bleed them again. I know: weird, and not so great for my patients. I did manage to get over the fainting spells as long as I didn't look when I was taking the blood sample, which was not an easy task; I had to insert the needle then look the other way. Most nurses have something that turns their stomach and mine just happened to be blood, needles, phlegm, and vomit ... oh, and feet ... and wounds. I was a great nurse though and I loved my patients; I just didn't like their bodily fluids!

The next time I saw the consultant from my interview was a few years later when I and another phlebotomist were messing about on the corridors in the hospital (we had these mad childish moments which kept us sane). I ran down the stairs ahead of my friend so I could hide and jump out on her. I heard her coming down the stairs and as she reached the bottom step, I jumped out loudly shouting, 'Boo!' with my arms up in the air for a greater effect. Yep, you guessed it, it wasn't her. The consultant, who was now quite elderly in years, got the full shock of my prank. He got such a fright that he jumped back. He leaned against the wall with his hands protectively across his heart (which must have been close to stopping) and he managed to mouth a feeble 'Ahhh!'.

'I'm so sorry,' I said. 'I thought you were someone else. Are you OK?'

He couldn't get away from me fast enough and scuttled off down the corridor.

Fortunately for me he must have been so embarrassed about the ordeal that nothing was ever said about it. I only saw him once more after that.

It was nearly Halloween and I decided to play a trick on the other phlebotomist. I had taken some little packets of tomato ketchup from the canteen and had emptied them out into a blood bottle. I waited for her to finish with a patient and, when I thought she was close enough, I opened the bottle and pretended to drink from it. I had ketchup around my mouth and on my fingers, and I went, 'Mmm', as if I was really enjoying it. When I turned around to see her reaction – oh my God, not again! It was the consultant. I tried to say 'It's Halloween – it's just ketchup' but he looked mortified and disgusted and once again, scuttled off without saying a word. I was sure I would be sacked for this but nothing ever came of it, thank God. This was the last time I ever saw him, something I'm grateful for!

I am sure many nurses have stories to share of situations that are funny, sad or even those they cannot fully explain. As well as some of the laughs I've had whilst working in the hospital, I have also had a few strange things happen when I have been on duty. One incident that springs to mind was when I had been nursing an overweight lady who had been admitted to hospital with breathing difficulties. She was so afraid she was going to die. I held her hand and told her she wasn't going to die, but she was still terrified and kept saying, 'I don't want to die. I'm so scared of dying.'

'You're not going to die' I told her, but she was frantic, breathless, and so *so* frightened.

We managed to sort her breathing out and a couple of hours later she sat by the side of her bed, still with her oxygen mask on, but breathing and talking normally, which was a relief. I was dealing with another patient when she shouted to me across the ward: 'Carolann, come here!'

She was breathing well, and this time she held my hands. She said, 'Thank you for looking after me, Carolann, but they have just been to visit me, and I am going to die very soon.'

I tried to say something but she stopped me.

'Don't worry though – I'm not scared anymore. I'm at peace and I am ready to go. It was beautiful.'

'You are not going to die,' I repeated.

This was a different woman to the one who had come into hospital only a couple of hours previously. She had been frightened and unable to breath but here she was, very relaxed and calm as she said to me in a gentle but firm manner,

'Carolann, please just listen to me, they have just been to see me, and I am not scared anymore. I just wanted to say thank you, but I am going to die very shortly, and I want you to know that I am OK with this, I am not scared anymore.'

I should have spent more time with her, asked her who had 'visited' her, but as is the story of most nurses' lives, we are just too busy. Regardless of who had 'visited' her that day, they had reassured and calmed her, which meant that when she died fifty minutes later from a massive heart attack, she was not feeling scared or anxious, which was some consolation for me. I have heard many patients say that they have had a 'visit' before they have died, and it's reassuring to know that this can put a patient's mind at ease before they pass away.

At times I have been acutely aware of the presence of a spiritual entity around me, even if I couldn't actually see it. I would get such a strong sensation that something was there, and have even felt a soft touch brush against me as well as experiencing some very strong smells. When I had cancer, I was aware of a very strong odour of cigarettes lingering all around me. It stayed with me no matter where I went. My car would smell of cigarettes and yet no one else around me could smell it. Even when I went to bed, I could smell it, and when you don't smoke and no one in the house smoked, the smell was even more pungent! It reminded me of the days when people used to be able to smoke in pubs. The next day your clothes and hair smelt like a dirty ashtray. Well, that was the smell that surrounded me at the time.

One day I went to see a fortune teller – not about the smell; I never considered it might be supernatural – more out of curiosity as I wanted to know about my health. The first thing she said to me was, 'You're surrounded by cigarette smoke' and she told me the names of the three people who were around me at that moment. They had all been chain smokers in life: Frankie, Frank and Francis and they were all family members who had passed. She said they were all looking after me, which I thought was nice. They have long since left now I am well again and on a different journey, but at least I discovered why I had the constant smell of cigarette smoke around me during that time. She told me everything was going to be OK and that I had nothing to worry about with my health, so that was also very encouraging, although I did get skin cancer some years later so maybe she wasn't quite as accurate as I first thought!

Old Man, Shadows and Strange Noises

So back to my dreams … about a year before I started this journey (which you, dear reader, will understand the more you read on), I began having strange dreams. These were of a confusing mixture, and sometimes I believed I was awake and actually seeing people in full colour in my house. It sounds OK, but believe me it wasn't – it was terrifying. Others involved a big black shadow I believed to be a man. He would cover my body with his own, so I would be paralysed in bed. One night I woke up (at least, I thought I was awake) and went into the spare room. I have no idea why but as I opened the door, I saw an old man get out of the bed. I remember thinking, who the hell are you? I could see all the details of his face and clothes clearly. He was very tall at least 6ft, and slightly bent over due to his old age. He had a good head of white hair and was fully clothed. He was wearing a white shirt tucked into black trousers with black braces. I could see all this detail clearly, including my spare room exactly as it was, (except there is not usually an old man sleeping in it!) Looking back, he reminded me a bit of the BFG (Big Friendly Giant). He came shuffling towards me. Now I don't know about you, but when something or someone starts to come at you, it's time to run. I was so scared, I ran down the hallway to my bedroom, looking behind me like they do in the horror films and he followed me, albeit very slowly. I tried to hit the light switch in my bedroom as he got closer, shuffling his feet, head down, but eyes firmly fixed on me. Shit! Shit! The light won't come on … it's not my light switch. It's not real – I'm asleep.

'WAKE UP … WAAAKE UP!' I shouted, and suddenly I was bolt upright in my bed dripping in sweat, my heart pounding. I was so happy to be awake and so relieved that it had only been a dream. But when I looked back at the door, Christ on a bike he was still there! There was nowhere to run as he was blocking the door. Then I saw it: the black shadow coming over my right shoulder and I knew my fate: paralysis. The old man stood watching me from the doorway as the black shadow enveloped me. And then I was gone once again into my world of bizarre and strange, terrifying dreams.

So, was I asleep or awake when I saw the old man? I don't know. I do know that my partner, Jed, described seeing this same man in our kitchen a few weeks later, when he had woken up in the early hours of the morning to get a drink. The old man had been leaning over our kitchen sink like he was washing dishes. Jed had also been terrified and ran straight back to the bedroom. He was as white as a ghost and looked really shaken up.

'What's the matter?' I said. 'You look like you've just seen a ghost.'

To which he replied, 'I think I just have!'

Welcome to my world, Jed!

These dreams were happening to me every night, so I began to keep a diary of them. I was exhausted with the restless nights and bedtime became something I wanted to avoid. Each night after finally falling asleep after hours of battling to stay awake, I would wake up (I think), and the black shadow would appear from behind me, always over my right shoulder. This shadow scared the hell out of me because I knew what was coming next. As the shadow came across my right shoulder it would start to paralyse me and I would try to get out of the bed to get away from it. It was always too quick however and I would only ever manage to half sit up before it enveloped me, pulling me back down into the supine position and once again I couldn't move. And then they would start: the very strange, frightening dreams or occurrences; I no longer knew what was real and what wasn't.

On two separate occasions after a visit from the black shadow man, I woke the following morning to find a large diagonal scratch across the right side of my back. The scratch was deep enough to leave a line of what I can only describe as a scab. It was as if someone or something had scratched me with a sharp object. The scratch wasn't there when I had gone to sleep, and it took a good week for it to disappear. It was only many months later following my surgery that I realised the scratch that had appeared in my sleep, was at the exact same location as the scar I now have on my back following my Mastectomy surgery.

On one particular night I was asleep when I was woken by a noise I can only describe as a 'Psst'. I heard it a few times in my right ear and used my right hand to brush the sound away, like swatting a fly. But it continued: 'Psst' until I woke up properly (I think), and as I looked over my right shoulder to see what had been making the noise, I saw the black shadow, which I now know was a man. Due to his shape and strength I was confident it was a male entity and so I'm going to call him the black shadow man. I was terrified, shouting, 'Nooo!' as I tried to get up but again, he was just too fast. He quickly came across my right shoulder, down my right breast and down my body, pinning me back down onto the bed. I was stuck in another nightmare, running around my house, waking up, not being awake, seeing things, scared senseless and trying desperately to wake up. Eventually I would wake up only to realise I was in fact still asleep. This pattern sometimes went on two or three times until I would eventually wake up properly. I would have to pinch myself to check I was really awake. The amount of times I believed I saw myself get out of bed and walk out my bedroom only to realise I was not actually doing it as I was asleep, was wearing me out. It was like Groundhog Day!

Each morning I would try and make sense of the madness of the dreams but not knowing which part was reality and which part was dream meant I was unable to make any sense, so I just made notes.

Wednesday 9th November 2011

The Dream That Saved My Life

I finally fell asleep after hours of desperately trying to avoid it. And then suddenly I was awake as normal, sitting up in bed in the semi-darkness. I turned to see the black shadow man over my right shoulder just before he enveloped me again. I felt paralysis set in as he weighed me down but tonight something was different: I didn't feel as scared. I went with it instead of trying to resist it. Straight away, this dream was different: I was not at home this time, unlike in all my other experiences. This time I was in a strange hospital, one that I wasn't familiar with. As a nurse I have worked in many hospitals, but I had never been in this one. I could see it all very clearly: I was looking after a patient who had a tumour. I had never worked on a cancer ward and therefore I'm not familiar with the specialised care required. The patient was lying on a bed, not quite horizontal, but slightly propped up with a pillow under their right shoulder. They had many drips attached to them, with fluids and antibiotics running through them and other attachments I wasn't familiar with. I was wearing a coat that was fastened up and this made me feel safe somehow. I pushed my hands deeper into my coat pockets. The coat was a sheepskin, tan in colour, and I felt it gave me some protection, even though I was in unfamiliar territory. I was wearing my comfy Ugg boots – strange attire to be wearing when nursing – why was I not in uniform? I only ever wore my Ugg boots when out walking on a Sunday. You know, those days when you can't be bothered and you just want to wrap up warm, be comfy and forget the boots with heels?

I watched my patient, wondering what I should do with them. I had no knowledge of cancer treatments and therefore, I was unsure what I was supposed to be monitoring. I looked into the patient's eyes and saw how terrified they were just as they started to fit. Then they died. The patient had kept eye contact with me throughout the fit and we just looked at each other, transfixed. I didn't call for help; I didn't do anything. I just stood there.

After they died, I tried to clean the room but there was water all over the floor, and I was standing in it. I felt like I was drowning. I was wading through the water but I was in over my head and I didn't know what to do.

I wandered down the hospital corridor, hands still stuffed tightly in my coat pockets, the collar still pulled high, trying to find some comfort and safety. Then I saw the ward sister, who I knew very well: Sister P. I heard her ask someone to pull the curtains around on another bay as another patient had just died. She asked me about my patient and I had to tell her they had also died. She asked, why have you let someone die when they only had a tumour?'

I was now crying, sitting on a double couch with her arm around me and facing a wall. (These little details are significant and I'll elaborate later on). I tell her I have no experience of nursing patients with tumours or cancer, so I don't know what I'm supposed to be looking for, or what I'm meant to be doing. I'm scared and tell her I don't want to look after another patient with a tumour as I don't have the skills.

Sister P tells me not to be scared about cancer, it could be beaten; no patient had to die and I'm not to worry about it. She says, 'There's another patient who has a tumour and you need to go back into the room and look after them.'

I try to explain again that I don't know how to nurse a patient with cancer but she just says in a firm but kind manner,

'You can look after someone with cancer. Check their pressures and make sure they're OK. You need to learn, and you will. Don't be scared, take control.' Then she sends me into a room with another patient to try again.

I was terrified; I knew I was out of my depth. As I walked into this strange but very vivid room, my coat tightly wrapped around me, I had an overwhelming feeling of fear, but I was determined I wouldn't be beaten by a tumour. I had to learn, and I *had* to save this patient. They were depending on me. I looked at my patient, who was staring straight into my eyes, and I suddenly felt as though I were looking into a mirror. This person was so frightened – I could see it in their eyes – and I didn't need to look at their body to know who I was looking at. Those frightened eyes staring back at me were the same eyes I had been looking at in the mirror for the last forty-two years!

At that moment I felt the black shadow lift from my body and I woke up gasping for breath. I didn't feel terrified like I normally did; I felt like I had lived the dream as a reality, rather than just dreamt it. It all felt so real – too real.

I woke my partner Jed and told him all about it. He was becoming used to me waking him at all hours and he patiently listened to what I had to say. I wrote it all down and drew sketches of what I had just seen and experienced. I can't draw very well so I just doodled little stick men and tried to keep the images in my head as best as I could, so that when I was awake properly in the morning, I could go over it all again.

Something was different about this dream and as I lay in my bed going over it all I realised that both the patients I had just dreamt about were me! But what was it all about? What did it all mean? There were two different outcomes and I knew which one I preferred …

It felt like I had been shown something, or perhaps had a warning. I had been given a choice: I could either deal with the patient with the tumour or let them die. Sister P had told me I had to learn about this condition. I just wasn't sure what it all meant, or if indeed it had a meaning at all.

Eventually I drifted off into a normal sleep, which was rare and unusual for me, and at long last I slept well for the rest of the night.

Throughout the next day the feelings of this dream just would not go away; it niggled at me. Sister P had lost her sister, who was also a friend of mine, to breast cancer and it had been a really sad time. I was working on the ward with Sister P the day her sister passed away. But that was many years ago, so surely the dream couldn't be linked to that episode? I couldn't make head or tail of it so I tried to put it to the back of my mind for the rest of the morning.

However, by lunchtime it was firmly back in the front of mind again. I could not shake off this uneasy feeling. Something was not right. It had all felt so real, and I was still reliving it. I was stood in the cupboard under the stairs sorting my washing out, like you do, and still thinking the dream through. I spent some time looking at my doodles, trying to make sense out of my dream, when I suddenly felt the need to check my breasts. I had never done this before; I had never felt the need. I was only young (which was a stupid thing to think as breast cancer can affect any woman or man – it's not ageist). So, I stopped what I was doing and, still under the stairs, I checked my breasts just to reassure myself that the dream wasn't a warning.

I wasn't even sure how to check my breasts, but it didn't take much. As soon as I felt my right breast there it was: a small lump, hardly noticeable unless you pressed your fingers in deep enough. I checked my left. Nope, nothing there. I asked Jed to feel it. Strangely, he joined me in the cupboard under the stairs with me. There wasn't much room and he had to duck down to fit in. He felt it and said he wasn't convinced it was anything serious. He said, he 'kinda felt something', but he was sure it was nothing. I immediately knew I didn't agree; my dream had to have been some sort of warning. I came out of the cupboard and booked an appointment at the doctors.

Friday 11th November 2011
One of The Worst Days of My Life to Date
Here we go: everyone on. The biggest rollercoaster ride in the country had just arrived in town with a seat right at the front for me. I hate rollercoasters at the best of times and would never normally get on one. I had an appointment for 9.20am to see the only doctor who was available: the one and only Dr Nasty. This doctor, as his name suggests, is not normally very nice. I am convinced that he won't be any good and I'll have to make another appointment to see someone else for a second opinion. He will brush it off as nothing – wait and see.

Anyway, I had a shower and shaved my armpits, as I knew he'd be sure to feel under them. Shortly after, I was sitting in the doctors' waiting room, patiently waiting to be called. All of a sudden everything around me was to do with breast cancer and I noticed it had been breast cancer awareness the previous month. They still had their posters up. Was this another sign?

I got called in for my appointment with two female junior doctors. This was not a good start; their faces said it all – they looked terrified. One sat on a chair to observe, while the other with her brand-new notebook and pencil started to ask questions.

'When was your last period?' she asked.

A good question to start with, I thought, but then she failed to ask if there was any history of breast cancer in my family, or if I had ever had breast implants. Was I on my period (as breasts can become lumpy at this time)?

Sometimes it's not great to be a nurse when you're on 'the other side'. I didn't think her assessment of my breast was that good; I did all the work for her – I even put her finger on the lump. 'The lump' is what it was now named – a bit like a pregnant woman calling her belly 'the bump'.

The doctor couldn't find the lump by herself. I know junior doctors all have to start somewhere but did it have to be on me, today? Any other time would have been fine, just not today. My nerves were already in tatters and I still had Doctor Nasty to argue with …

She didn't bother to check the rest of the breast or feel under my armpits. She didn't even check my left breast. I could have had loads of lumps and bumps, for all she knew. She was very much out of her depth and, as much as I didn't want her spindly fingers touching my armpit, she really should have done this as part of her assessment. As a nurse you can usually tell when a junior doctor is fresh out of medical school, you can tell if they've never had their hands on a patient; that fear is always in their eyes. With their crisp white jackets and stethoscopes, you would see them all arrive on the ward looking lost and scared. I couldn't blame them – being throw in at the deep end is a big responsibility.

My advice to any new junior doctors is always be nice to the nurses you work with as they may just save your arse one day. And if you're nice to the nurses, they in return will help you and make your life on the ward so much easier.

It must have been a shock having to touch a stranger's boob, at least, they gave me the impression it was, and so the armpit was a definite no-go area to them. When I asked the other student if she wanted to have a feel, I had hardly finished the sentence when she replied rather bluntly, 'No.' She looked horrified that I had even asked. I thought it was a good opportunity for her to feel a breast with a lump and she should have taken it. You have to learn somehow. She told me she would run this past the doctor – that's what they had to do with each patient they saw. They both appeared quite nervous and the nerves were contagious. Whilst waiting to see Doctor Nasty I had noticed when I first came into the surgery, he walked past me, ignoring me and the other patients, and when another younger doctor said good morning to him, he didn't even acknowledge it. He looked so mean. I even texted Jed to tell him how fierce and rude this doctor was and that I would have to come back again later for a second opinion with a different doctor. I had my speech all prepared because there's nothing worse than being caught off guard; in hindsight you always wish you had said this or that, so I was making sure I had an answer for anything he might say to me. I would never normally see Doctor Nasty. In fact, I'd rather suffer than see him. Well, when he is rude and tells me in his unprofessional manner that 'it's nothing but a fatty lump' and I'm 'worrying over nothing', he's going to get it. Bring it on Doctor Nasty!

I was left alone in the examination room for what felt like ages whilst the two novices went to speak to Doctor Nasty. Then the door opened wide and in he walks with the two junior doctors like puppies at his heel. He told me to sit on the bed and strip to the waist. No good morning, no niceties, just sit on the bed and strip off. (It's the story of my life!) The two juniors watched as if they'd suddenly developed a keen interest in the situation.

He asked me where the lump was, but I already had my finger on the spot to show him. I know exactly where the lump is even though I have only had it for a day. He examined the breast and said, 'Erm, right, OK. Get dressed and take a seat in the waiting room.'

I should have realised then it was not good news. Surely if it were, he would have said, 'it's nothing to worry about,' and sent me on my way. He opened the door and all three of them walked out into the waiting room. Meanwhile, I was still sitting there with both breasts hanging out and he hadn't closed the curtains! A nurse would have closed the curtains and given me some time and privacy to get dressed.

Luckily for me, the patients outside (apart from one man who quickly looked away – thank you) looked up at the doctor and not at me, so I was spared the humiliation of being seen half naked. I quickly tried to cover up and keep whatever dignity I had. Little did I know this dignity was soon to be hidden away in a dark cupboard, somewhere I would never be able to find it again. These boobs were soon to become as popular and as frequently ogled as Jordan's! If only I was paid as much as her!

Alone in the examination room, I got dressed and then went back to the waiting room for what seemed like ages. It was still busy and the man who had caught a sneaky peak at my wonderful breasts was still waiting, which was a bit awkward as you can imagine. We avoided eye contact and he was called in to see the doctor just a few minutes later.

I checked my watch and realised they had kept me waiting twenty minutes. What was going on? I texted Jed again to tell him what was happening and that I was really worried. He was also worried. If there wasn't a problem, if Doctor Nasty thought it was just a fatty lump or cyst, he would have sent me away by now. (I would have promptly rebooked with another, nicer doctor for a second opinion on the way out!)

Then, finally, the door opened, and Doctor Nasty called me in. Straight away I saw it: a crisp white letter in his hand and I knew this was not going to be good news. The white envelope contained a referral letter and that was what had taken so long to sort out – he had been writing the letter. The two junior doctors stood in silence and as I looked at them, they put their heads down. Even Doctor Nasty, who didn't ordinarily show any outward sign of concern or sympathy was now looking at me with … yes, you got it, concern and sympathy. I didn't know this kind side of Doctor Nasty, and I didn't want concern or sympathy. I wanted to be told 'it's just a fatty lump – you're worried over nothing'.

The doctor spoke: 'Yes, you do indeed have a lump, it is not a cyst but a fixed lump. We will send you to the hospital for tests as no woman should have a lump.'

He told me he was not too worried, but it was best to get it checked out just in case. The referral could take up to two weeks. He told me the lump was the size of a pea, maybe bigger. My mind was whirling, thinking of peas and the size it could be depending on the type. Garden peas are small … processed a bit bigger … and then Marrowfat even bigger still. The lump only felt small and I was shocked. He asked me if I had any questions and I shook my head. I couldn't exactly ask him what pea he was comparing it to. He told me the hospital would be in touch within the next two weeks. Shit! I had not been expecting this. Can you get off a roller coaster when it is moving this fast?

I felt numb. I sat in my car and, holding back the tears, I phoned Jed and told him: 'It's real. I have got a lump.'

Ten minutes later I was at home, still feeling numb. I didn't even take my coat off. It was the same coat from my dream and keeping it on gave me the comfort I needed. It felt like I was being hugged by my mum and I pulled the coat up over my neck and sank as far into it as I could. For the first time in my life I was scared and I sat and cried, feeling very sorry for myself.

I didn't cry for long though – it was not in my nature and I decided to take some action and sort this out once and for all. I didn't have to wait two weeks and I was not prepared to wait, so I decided to tackle it head on and I booked an appointment at the private hospital close by for the following Monday morning. The scan was booked for 9am then at 9.50am I would see a consultant. They quoted me £185 to have the tests, see the consultant and receive the results – all within a few hours, or so they had told me, which I thought was great. But by the time I put the phone down I was crying so much I could hardly speak. I never cried. I wasn't sure I knew *how* to cry let alone if I had the correct waterworks to be able to cry. Anyway, it turns out I do have, and I can. And this time there was no stopping.

My father arrived at the house in what was great but bizarre timing. He hardly ever came to the house, but I was delighted to see him and I broke down crying as he hugged me, telling me over and over again that it was going to be all right. People always say it's going to be all right but deep down, and after my dream, I knew this was just the start of a journey that would take me on one hell of a ride of ups and downs, testing every emotion.

I looked at the clock and realised it was 11am on the 11th September 2011. Whilst most people were honouring the one-minute silence, I was crying my heart out and being comforted by my dad. And all the time I was wrapped up in my coat, which was soon to become my second skin, providing me with the comfort of a safety blanket throughout the journey, just like in my dream.

After a spell of feeling very sorry for myself I had to pull myself together as I was meeting my best friend at the Trafford Centre. Despite the situation I decided to go and managed to go through the motions of shopping and having lunch. I held my tears in throughout. I wanted to scream to the other happy shoppers that I might have cancer. I looked normal and healthy, no one would ever have known. I was only 42 years old – why was I even having to think about something like this? I wanted to get off the roller coaster but knew I had to stay on till the end. That's life: full of ups and downs.

Thinking back to my dream I knew I must not be the patient who died. I had to be the one that survived. My friend told me not to worry but it was hard not to, and as I walked back through the shopping centre on my own, I had to use every bit of strength not to break down and cry. I couldn't believe those bloody tears – there must have been forty-two years' worth of tears and emotions waiting to come out! It's strange how life can throw you without any warning: one minute your life is perfect, and you have no other decisions to make apart from what to have for tea or where to go on holiday. This journey was about to dictate everything from what I ate, to when I slept to what I could do on a day-to-day basis. Never take for granted what you have in life. Always be thankful for everything. Look at the blue sky, hear the birds singing, be thankful for your health, and your wealth – regardless of how much you have. Be thankful you can walk, talk and hear. There's so much to be thankful for and yet we take it all for granted. Never again will I do this, and each and every day I thank the universe for everything I have in life.

But back then, before I could see life so clearly, things were just getting worse. It was horrible. I had to tell my daughter, my beautiful loving daughter, whom I always try to protect. She's my best friend and ally; I tell her everything, so this has to be done.

I cry, she cries, we hug. She says she has never seen me cry before and that upsets her even more. I decide not to tell my son, who is in London, not till I get my results and my reasoning is this:

1) He is not here so can't see what is going on. What's the point of upsetting another child if there is nothing he can do?

2) The results may come back negative. We can live in hope.

I cling onto hope. My daughter is aware of my hospital visit. We live across the road from each other, we work together, and we are so close there is no way I can hide this from her. She would smell a rat. But by God, it was one of the hardest things I have ever had to do. And this was the only time (that I know of) that she cried throughout this journey. She is tough like her mum, but that's not always a good trait.

Black Shadow Man

Well some good news: the rollercoaster was on its way up (exactly the opposite of what I would normally call good; as you know, I hate roller coasters and going up is just as terrifying as going down. I prefer being down or not being on it at all.) It also looked like the black shadow man had gone. This was all very strange.

The final dream I had of black shadow man was that I was woken up by a noise coming from my living room. At least I think I had woken up. I remember walking across the landing. My heart had started to beat faster and I could hear it pulsating loudly in my ears and chest, I was terrified once again. Yet I still managed to walk down the stairs and into the living room. It felt like a scene from a scary movie where they hear a noise and instead of waking their partner up, they choose to head off alone to find out what the noise is and all with no lights on! Why do people never learn? Yet here I was doing exactly the same.

As I opened the living room door, there he was: the black shadow man. Only this time he was outside in the garden, not in the house. His tall black frame looked threatening and imposing. I could make no facial features out but could see he was a solid mass of what looked like thick black smoke, only in the shape of a person – a man. I say solid as his outline was sharp so you could make out his shape, but his actual body looked smoky and swirly, if that makes sense. His body was pressed against the outside of the window and he was banging hard with his fists against the glass pane. The glass was bending and bowing like a piece of bendy plastic and he used both fists at the same time to hammer against the glass. Despite that, I suddenly realised that no matter what force he used, he could not get in and I watched for a few moments to make sure.

I was still very much afraid but I could see he was now on the outside and unable to get to me. Was he the reality of my cancer? The thing I was now facing up to? Perhaps there was no use for him anymore as I was now too strong.

As he continued to bang at the window, I started to move away, just in case I was wrong, and he did get back in. I didn't want to take any chances and I certainly didn't want to have to run if he managed to break the glass.

Before heading back to bed, I felt the need to check the back door was locked. I was terrified as I had an image in my head that as I put my hand on the door handle to check it was closed, someone on the outside would open it at the same time, and it would be someone I wouldn't want to see. (I watch far too many scary films even though

I don't like them). My heart was palpitating as I walked in darkness through the kitchen towards the back door. Have you ever made your heart beat so loudly you can hear it on the outside? That was all I could hear in the quiet of my house: my heart strong, fast, and loud. I slowly reached my hand out to grab the handle.

Please please do not let it be open and please please do not let there be someone standing there!

I pulled the handle down and with a huge sense of relief I realised it was locked and quickly ran back to bed. Had I been asleep or had this all actually happened? I really didn't know; I could not distinguish reality from fiction anymore. Even as I got back into bed, I could see Jed was sleeping peacefully, and my room appeared normal. My side of the bed was empty, with the quilt pulled back from when I had got out. I settled back into my bed and closed my eyes.

There were no further bad dreams of this sort, ever. And there have been no more visits from the black shadow man.

I was still worried sick about my health however, and I struggled to sleep every night because of that, but each time I did finally manage to get to sleep, I slept well with no strange dreams and didn't wake again until the morning. This was so strange as I'd had almost a year of not sleeping due to bad dreams. Then suddenly, I found out about the lump and hey presto! The dreams suddenly stopped.

The black shadow man has never come back to visit me since and I have never felt his presence since that night. I still believe *he* was the cancer. He was always on my right shoulder and breast, and he only left when I acknowledged the lump and began to fight back and take control.

Many years later, I saw a programme about nurses who had ghost stories to tell. This particular nurse told a story about a black shadow man whom she described in the exact same way as 'my' black shadow man. She said she had spoken to him and he told her he was the Angel of Death. She said that as scary as he appeared, he actually made death seem a calm and gentle experience.

My heart raced on hearing this as I really felt it was the same figure who had haunted my dreams years before. She described seeing him come as a large black shadow and wrap himself over her patient. So, was my black shadow man actually the Angel of Death? Had he come to me to warn me about my cancer because it wasn't my time to go? Perhaps he had been hoping to take me but my spirit guides decided it wasn't my time to go, and therefore warned me of my fate.

Thinking it might have been the Angel of Death visiting me on those occasions terrifies me more than the black shadow man! Just listening to this nurse made my heart race and my stomach sick with nerves. I knew we had both experienced the same phenomenon and, as much as I don't like to admit it, I really do believe it was the Angel of Death, also known as the Grim Reaper. Now that's a scary thought! I'd woken up to a few strange-looking people in my life, but none as scary as him!

12th November 2011

So, I had forty-eight hours to keep my mind occupied and there was only one place I could keep busy and active and forget all my worries: the family business, Debut Academy of Performing Arts. I didn't tell too many people at the school about the lump, as I didn't want to look stupid if it turned out to be a false alarm. Deep down though I knew it wasn't a false alarm. I felt really tired, which was very unusual for me. It must be all the emotional, crying stuff – I'm just not used to it. What I am good at though is plastering a smile on my face and putting on a show. I am very good at hiding my emotions, or at least I think I am. I have learnt over the years never to judge someone by their actions or how they speak to you. If someone is rude or abrupt or snaps at you, take a step back before retaliating; you never know what that person is dealing with in life, or how they are coping with it. I was walking around with what felt like the weight of the world on my shoulders but no one could see that. All my customers and students could only see me as my usual happy and chatty self. If only they knew I was frightened, feeling sick with worry, and hiding the fact that I might have cancer.

13th November 2011
The Calm Before the Storm
It was a busy weekend at the dance school, we had exams, and this kept me occupied. One of my customers, who I had mentioned my concerns to, told me not to worry. She had had a similar scare and her lump, which they'd removed, had turned out to be just a cyst. However, I couldn't help thinking that according to Doctor Nasty, it wasn't just a cyst and, on some level, I knew it was something more sinister.

Exam day kept me very busy and the time flew by. In fact, it went too fast for my liking. I knew that once the day was over, I would have to start facing reality once again. As each hour passed, I was brought closer and closer to the next morning when examinations and scans would begin.

Who would have thought that hospital life with all the examinations, scans and tests would soon become second nature to me and be as much a part of my everyday life as going to work each day?

Our older students were so worried about their exams and I envied them; if only this was all I had to worry about. All our students passed and got great results, as always. This was one thing in life that is always a certainty. We teach well and the students always do brilliantly and make us proud. Watching our students as they waited in line to take their exams, all smart and professional-looking, made me feel so proud. For a good ten hours most of my fears and worries were forgotten as I concentrated on keeping our students calm. It was so tranquil and peaceful as the last few students entered the studio for their exam. Little did I know this was to be the calm before the storm.

I was tired by the time I got home, but I suddenly had a strong urge to speak to my mum, who was living in Spain. I felt like a child desperate for their mum to make them feel better and to make all their fears and worries go away. I yearned to see her or at least speak to her, but I was worried if I told her what was going on, she would be so concerned she'd be on the first flight home. And if my results turned out negative then the trip would have been a waste of time and energy for her. I broke down. I was torn between my natural urge to speak to my mum and sparing her feelings. Jed said, 'if you need your mum then phone her.' I *did* need her, more now than ever. I felt like I had regressed to being a small child again. I just needed my mum to make it all better.

I did try to phone her that evening, but I was so emotional I could not bring myself to speak to her. I dialled her number but hung up before it even got a chance to ring. What was wrong with me? Jed redialled the number as I was now inconsolable. And then there she was on the other end of the phone. I heard her beautiful, soft, caring voice, which made me even more upset and I couldn't speak (it's not often I'm lost for words!) Jed comforted me and told my mum everything. I still couldn't speak to her.

Eventually I pulled myself together enough to phone her back. It was hard but I kept it together as much as I could.

My dear mother said, 'It doesn't matter what the outcome is; if it's negative then that's great news. It doesn't matter if I come home and it's negative – that's what we want. This is what families do. They give hugs and support when needed, regardless. And if you need a hug then I will come home. You will not deal with this alone.'

I sat with my coat on – my comfortable security blanket – as I listened to her gentle, caring words.

All night I slept fitfully, tossing and turning, praying for night to become day. I was so weary; all this crying and emotion was making me physically and mentally exhausted. Lying in the dark unable to sleep was doing me no favours as it allowed my mind too much time to think, and it was going into overdrive. What would tomorrow bring? If only I could sneak a peek into the future ... then again, if I had seen what the future had in store for me, I would have decided to stay firmly in the past!

Monday 14th November 2011

Here we go the rocky road of ups and downs ...
We drove in silence to the private hospital (when I am nervous, I don't like to speak). The hospital was able to

give me my results straight away, which was the reason I was going private. It was going to be worth every penny for my peace of mind.

The traffic was awful, but we still managed to arrive at the hospital for 9am on the dot. Jed had taken the day off work to be with me, and my mum was due home later that day. I just hoped we'd get some good news to tell her.

On arrival at reception, I was greeted by a friendly smiley-faced lady, who took my name and turned back to her computer to find my appointment. After a couple of minutes tapping away and re-checking my name twice, her face changed from a smile to concern.

'I'm sorry' she said, 'I can't find any appointments for a mammogram or any other procedure under your name. Could you have booked it under another name?'

Why do they ask that? As if I would book it under a different name. What's the point in having your own name and booking appointments in another? This is not the GUM Clinic (the sexual health clinic) where I might want to remain anonymous!

She advised me to go straight up to X-ray on the first floor in case they had received my paperwork there. But you guessed it ... they had no knowledge of me there either. What a great start! The receptionist there told me I couldn't have a mammogram without a consultant's authority so I was sent back down to the main reception.

The receptionist there didn't know what to do with me so she quickly sent me to another reception area to see if they had me booked in there by mistake. It was clear she was passing the buck and perhaps thought I was about to lose my patience and kick off.

I explained yet again (to the third receptionist) that I was supposed to be booked in for a mammogram, a scan and to see the consultant at 9.50am for the results. But nothing was showing on the computer and, without the authority of a consultant, no one could help me. Nothing is ever straightforward for me and I must have the patience of a saint…

Then the third receptionist found me on the system and said I was booked into see a consultant, (yes, I knew that, that is what I had been saying for the last half hour), but he had not signed any forms for me to have the tests and without the signed appropriate forms … (yes, I know I could not have a mammogram). And as for the scan, well they didn't do scans on a Monday as it's not a one-stop breast clinic day, Tuesday's are, so I couldn't have that done anyway. I understood that. It had been said to me enough times. Maybe they should let the department that booked me in for today know, so they knew for the future.

I was told to take a seat in the waiting room; the consultant might be able to sort it out once he arrived. I felt sick with anticipation and withdrew into myself desperate once again for some security. My coat was wrapped tightly around me just like in my dream. But I was sure this was not the hospital from my dream. Maybe that was a blessing in disguise; perhaps my dream was not becoming a reality.

Time ticked on and there was still no sign of the consultant. I watched the other patients come and go and as quickly as the waiting room filled up, it emptied again. The receptionist kept trying to contact him but could not get through.

9.50am came and went and there was still no sign of him. Jed's leg was bouncing up and down as he was getting anxious or impatient – I'm not sure which – but it was making me feel even more nervous, so much so I couldn't even form a sentence to ask him to sit still. I just put my hand firmly on his leg to hold it steady and he got the message. I didn't want any noise or movement, I just needed to sit very quietly and still until I saw the consultant. This was my coping mechanism.

I asked the receptionist to keep trying to get hold of him; I wasn't leaving till I saw him. And so, the waiting game began ... Thankfully I am a very patient person, stubborn and determined but very patient.

An hour later I was called into a room by a very sympathetic nurse, who kept apologising for the consultant not turning up. I told her it wasn't her fault. She couldn't believe how calm and polite I was and actually said, 'I can't understand why you aren't shouting at me.'

Shouting was not going to change the situation or make the consultant magically appear. Besides, by that point I was so numb and exhausted, I couldn't shout at her if I tried. The build-up to this day had been massive and I thought I'd have had my scans and received the results by now. The receptionist and the nurse had tried everything to get hold of the consultant. They were doing their best and I appreciated all their help. They advised me to go home and said they would rebook me in for an appointment the following day when the breast clinic was running. I firmly said, 'No'.

I had to see someone and I wouldn't leave until I saw a consultant. The nurse persisted; there were no other breast surgeons working that day but I was adamant: I was not budging and told her she had to get someone to see me.

'You have to keep trying to get hold of him,' I told

her. 'I have made an appointment to see a consultant and I will not leave until I do.'

I couldn't believe this was happening to me, but I was determined that I would sit there all day until I saw someone. I can be very determined and stubborn.

The nurse relented and sat us in a side room, so we were not out in the reception. She could see I was getting upset and I don't think she wanted me to cause a scene. There was no danger of that; I had no energy left to shout or cause a scene. It wasn't like me but then I didn't feel like me at that moment. I was there to have tests and see a specialist and by God that was what I was going to do!

She asked someone to make us a cup of tea. A good old cup of English tea always helps in a crisis. Keep calm and drink tea. She told them to bring biscuits too and whispered,

'We wouldn't normally give you biscuits; we're not allowed to. Because it's a private hospital you usually have to pay for them, so you're lucky.'

Jeez, I didn't feel very lucky. Never mind me not getting a scan or a mammogram or seeing a consultant, all of which I was paying for, I've got biscuits and tea, so all is good in the world again!

The biscuits when they came were Bourbon creams in those little packs of three but they were all broken. Funny the little details you remember. These must have been the discarded biscuits and that's why we'd been given them. I presume private patients get to eat them whole, especially if they've paid full price for them. Bless the NHS: they give you biscuits no questions asked and a sandwich or piece of toast.

I told the nurse to ring around other private hospitals

to find me an appointment for the same day. This was their fuck up, excuse the French, and they needed to sort it out. She was very nice and said she would, but she had to be very careful. Because it was a private hospital, she wasn't allowed to phone other hospitals and make appointments for patients – it was all to do with the money. But she was upset for me, as she had had a breast cancer scare a few years previously so she knew how I felt.

'I'll try and get you an appointment at another hospital, but if I hang up suddenly it's because my manager has walked in.'

She was certainly going the extra mile for me. Just as she picked up the phone and dialled, another nurse walked in (without knocking – lucky I was dressed) and said, 'Good news! We've managed to get hold of the consultant.'

Thank the Lord! I was so happy. Apparently, he had been stuck in theatre with one of his NHS patients, which is why he had not been answering his phone. Now I know all patients should be treated the same, but I had booked an appointment to see him and I was paying for his time, so he really should learn to manage it better. Eventually I was to find out this specialist was an angel who he did things his own way.

They told me he would now see me at 4.30pm. What a relief! I had been due to see him at 9.50am so … six-and-a-half hours later. Still, better late than never and I was just so relieved I would get to see him after all. Little did I realise at the time, but this was to be the first of many highs and lows that would test my patience throughout my journey.

Another lady, who had also been waiting to see this consultant, had made the decision to go home and return the following day. I just couldn't do that. My frame of mind wouldn't allow it and my determination had paid off.

The consultant had requested a mammogram and scan before I was to see him at 4.30pm so I was sent back up to the X-ray department to book a time for the scan, only for the receptionist to tell me I couldn't have a scan as there was no radiologist available on a Monday. FFS (more French)! I felt at any moment a camera crew would pop out and say, 'You've been framed!' All I could have was a mammogram which:

1) Cost me more than double the price originally quoted

2) Made me go quite dizzy.

I had never had a mammogram before and didn't realise that it would be quite so uncomfortable. Have you ever had a mammogram? If not, I don't want to put you off, but they squeeze and stretch your boob as if they're kneading and stretching bread dough. I never knew my boob was that pliable! Then they position your boob into a machine which resembles two flat iron plates, (the procedure resembles some sort of mediaeval torture), which close together and flatten your boob so you are stuck, unable to move. Your lovely round boob is now as flat as a pancake. (I remember hoping it would go back to its original shape afterwards).

As a child I used to watch a programme called *Barbapapa* about a creature that resembled a blob and could change its form into different shapes. It was a kids' TV show in the 70s and is worth a Google. Anyway, this programme sprang to mind. You could never inflict this shape on your boob at home. In fact, they should give a safety warning of Do Not Try This at Home. Your arm is stretched up and around to hold onto the machine and you have to bend your neck backwards and turn your head to the side. It helps if you are flexible or a contortionist. And with me being so short, I had to stand on my tiptoes, so my boob was not further stretched. It was then the nurse asked, 'Are you comfortable?'

Then they realise that not every part of your boob is in the machine so they give it a further stretch and you get that feeling when you give birth – you know, the one where you feel the final stretch of the baby's head coming out, and they say pant. You think, here we go: the skin is about to tear ... well, that's the feeling during the final stretch of your boob for a mammogram. It felt like a Chinese burn. And then I went dizzy and nearly passed out. I was traumatised, and they had to give me water and let me sit down for a bit. I've always been crap at all this: no good with blood tests and now no good with mammograms. Let's hope this meant the end of the tests.

How your boob goes back to its normal shape after being squeezed flat is beyond me, but it did. As soon as it was released it quickly returned to its original shape, a bit like a memory foam pillow. The body is so very clever. I was also surprised it wasn't left with any stretch marks. Who would have known that the boob was so pliable, tough, strong, and resilient! No wonder women are the stronger sex. Wouldn't you think that God would have made our vaginas out of boob material so they could stretch without tearing during childbirth, and pop back into place instead of leaving us with sagging bums and low-hanging vaginas which leak urine every time we sneeze or laugh?

The nurse carrying out the mammogram said she

couldn't see anything sinister, (which seemed strange) though the consultant would confirm that with me later, but they were not concerned. The nurses were really nice. They booked me in for a scan for the following morning, just in case the consultant wanted one.

To pass some time until we saw the consultant, we headed to the canteen for lunch. But I had no appetite. My stomach was a flurry of dancing butterflies and knots, which meant there was no room for food, so we decided to head to town to try and pass some time wandering around the shops. Our minds were not really on shopping which was unusual for us. Once again, I was watching the other shoppers, who all looked like they had no cares in the world. Yet here was I with what felt like the weight of the world on my shoulders. It was cold and we decided to head back to the hospital to wait. I just wanted to be there, ready for the consultant; I couldn't concentrate on anything else.

We still had lots of time to pass so first we had a cup of tea in the canteen, then moved to the reception area where we sat in silence for an hour, before moving to another waiting area near the consulting rooms and sat there for another hour, again mostly in silence. I felt so sick. Jed's leg started twitching as he began getting nervous, and I had to put my hand on his leg to make him sit still again. I was feeling on edge and so so nervous. I sat transfixed by the clock counting each minute. *Come on consultant – you've kept me waiting for hours!* I discovered that the more you watch a clock the slower it appears to move – just like a watched kettle never boils.

A Close Call

At bloody last! At 4.30pm the consultant called me in to see him. He was a very nice man, average height with dark hair and very smartly dressed. He shook our hands firmly and introduced himself. I'll call him 'Matt' to protect his identity. He apologised for keeping us waiting for so long, confirming he got caught up in theatre with one of his NHS patients. I was tempted to complain and tell him it wasn't good enough; that I'm so worried and stressed out but you don't, do you? We were just so relieved that we had finally got to see him; he was actually standing in front of us at last! So, we just smiled, and before I knew it, the following words fell out of my mouth: 'Oh that's fine – don't worry, we weren't doing anything else.'

WTF!

The consultant examined my breasts then told me to

get dressed and take a seat at his desk. He told me he had seen my mammogram and it was negative, which was great, and along with the examination he had just performed he was happy the lump was nothing sinister. Good news!

Now, most people would just have just taken these results as gospel and left the hospital thinking they were in the clear. A negative mammogram, a thorough examination and reassurance from a consultant would have satisfied most people. Only, I'm not most people. And had I been one of these people, I wouldn't be here today. I would have lost my life to breast cancer. It's a very frightening thought and I am so thankful for my life-saving dream and so thankful that I was determined, stubborn and thorough regarding which tests I wanted. Thank God I didn't take no for an answer.

'How certain are you that this is nothing sinister?' I asked.

'I'm 80% positive it's just a lump – non-cancerous.'

'Will you remove it?' I asked him.

'Why go through an operation when you don't need one? I am not worried – your mammogram was negative and shows no sign of a cancer,' he replied.

So, he was happy for me to go home, confident it was nothing serious.

I persisted: 'What about the scan I have booked for tomorrow?'

'I'll cancel that for you. You don't need a scan,' came his reply.

Now I know you think I should have been jumping for joy, what with the negative result and positive conversation with the consultant. The dream had been wrong, or confused perhaps. But it was my dream that brought me here in the first place and something still didn't feel right. Firstly, this wasn't the hospital from my dream and secondly, my gut didn't agree with the consultant.

I told him a little of my dream and said, 'I still want my scan in the morning. 80% is not 100%. There's still a 20% chance that you're wrong.'

Eventually, he realised I was not going to be dissuaded.

'You're not going to be happy until you get a scan, are you? And you're not going to take no for an answer,' he said.

'No, I'm not. My dream was too real to ignore.'

He relented and agreed I could go ahead with the scan in the morning. And that was that. All that waiting to be told it was nothing. So why did I still feel sick to my stomach and not relieved? He shook hands again and told us not to worry: *it was good news.*

We left the hospital with Jed feeling relieved. He said that the consultant was so laidback and reassuring, he was happy to go along with his diagnosis. Eighty per cent was a good result and the consultant was very convincing that everything was OK. He didn't appear worried at all.

I didn't share his enthusiasm and I didn't feel relieved. Eighty per cent wasn't bad odds but it wasn't 100%. And something still didn't feel right … I kept remembering my dream and although the consultant said there was nothing to worry about, I didn't share the same thoughts. I was listening to my gut, which had never let me down yet. My gut was telling me to stay focused on my dream, even though I would have preferred not to.

We got a nice bottle of wine and some tapas for tea and Jed toasted me for the great result. I went along with the charade, but I didn't feel reassured. I updated my daughter and let my son know what had been happening. He was shocked but glad it had turned out OK at the hospital. My lovely mum arrived home, which was just wonderful. Her advice was that I shouldn't have a lump in my breast and therefore I should ask the consultant about having it removed, which would make her happier. I resolved to discuss this with the consultant the following day. I slept a bit better that night. I just hoped my hospital visit would go more smoothly than that day's!

Tuesday 15th November 2011
Fight or Flight
By the morning Jed was not feeling very well. He had the start of 'man flu', so I told him to stay at home. It was only a scan I was going for, so it wouldn't take too long. And as he said, we knew the outcome anyway; the scan was just a precaution.

By the way, did you know 'man flu' is a real thing? We joke about it but men actually experience flu differently from women. It's true! Women still suffer more, but we have to humour the men, and so I told Jed to put his feet up and take it easy until I got home.

Mum came with me to the hospital and we were taken in on time, which was great. The doctor carrying out the scan explained that lots of woman feel lumps and they usually turn out not to be nothing to worry about. He had seen my mammogram and spoken to the consultant and was not expecting to see anything sinister. This scan was really just to confirm the original diagnosis. I felt as if he didn't believe I actually had a lump. But I knew I did. It was very easy to find, and once I had mastered exactly where it was, I couldn't stop touching it to check it was still there!

I lay on the bed and he began to scan my right breast. There was a large TV screen on the wall so I could see what he was picking up. My mum was standing next to me, also watching. It reminded me of when you get a scan when you are pregnant, and you get to see your baby on the screen for the first time. Except, hey presto! I got to see my lump on the screen. It sat there, staring menacingly back at us all. The doctor's face said it all: he was so shocked. He looked at me and for a split second I could see a sympathetic look in his eyes. He said, 'I'm so sorry, you were right. There is a lump and it does look suspicious.'

Shit. I knew it but it didn't bring me any pleasure being proved right. My mum took my hand and looked at me. I was absolutely shitting myself. He scanned under my armpit then moved back to the lump. It looked more like a mini marshmallow than the pea described by Doctor Nasty. Maybe it had grown in the previous five days.

He told me I needed a biopsy and that he could do that now, rather than me having to come back again. This was all happening way too fast, but I didn't have time to think about it. He pulled a trolley towards me. It was covered with a green surgical cloth so I had no idea what was lurking underneath. When he pulled the cover back, I was presented with lots of shiny strange-looking surgical instruments and it made me want to pass out. I could feel and hear my heart beating in my chest and I desperately wanted to let Jed know what was happening. I needed time to digest all of this information and to prepare myself.

I looked back at the instruments, all shiny and menacing,

and the doctor was already gowning up as if he were about to carry out an operation on me. I noticed a scalpel among the gleaming instruments and I thought, *I can't do this*. I was going to pass out ... my head was spinning, my heart was racing and my fight or flight urge was kicking in, only it was more flight than fight! I looked at my mum and said, 'I can't do this.'

She held my hand and said, 'Yes you can. Everything will be OK.'

Her lovely gentle voice was so reassuring, her hands were so soft and I knew that with my mum at my side I could face anything life could throw at me. My mum: my guardian angel. So, I closed my eyes and tried to block the nightmare out. If I couldn't see what was happening, then maybe I wouldn't be so scared. I try to get into my own little world where everything was peaceful and calm and I had no worries. I lay on the bed, concentrating on my breathing, with my eyes closed and my mum holding my hand. *OK, I can do this ....*

Then they spoiled it all by asking an assistant nurse to come in and hold my hand. She moved my mum to the bottom of the bed so she could get close to me. WTF! I didn't want this bloody stranger holding my hand! I wanted my mum. Why didn't I say anything? Everything was suddenly out of my control; the calm, tranquil feeling I had created was suddenly shattered by her taking my hand. And besides, I didn't appreciate her fake smile and the stupid questions like, 'Are you going anywhere nice on your holidays this year?'

This wasn't the bloody hairdressers! I was about to have a medical procedure performed on my boob *and* I had just found out I may have cancer. FUCK OFF!

I couldn't speak. No words would come out. And so, she continued to hold my hand, oblivious to how upset this small gesture was making me feel. I tried to shake my hand free, wriggle my fingers out of hers, but she had such a good grip that I couldn't release myself. I had my right arm up behind my head and then the procedure began …

The doctor told me to keep nice and still, so I couldn't free myself of the nurse clinging to me. I wanted to scream, 'STOP A MINUTE!' so I could get myself together, take back some control and let my dear mother take her rightful place next to me. But I was frozen, paralysed with fear.

I didn't even answer the daft questions from the nurse, and I heard my mum explain my silence: 'She is being quiet as this is how she likes to cope. She's relaxing.'

The doctor began the procedure by cleaning the skin on my boob. He said, 'sharp scratch coming up' as he injected the anaesthetic to numb the area. I felt so apprehensive and lightheaded. I'd had no time to get my head around any of it and felt totally out of control. It wasn't what I'd been expecting from the appointment; I thought it would just be a scan and then I would wait for the results. Instead, I felt like I was drowning – I couldn't breathe – and I just wanted to make a run for it.

The doctor said he was just about the make a cut. WTF! These are words I DO NOT want to hear at any time! I told him not to tell me what he was doing – I didn't want to know. But he claimed he had to tell me, so I didn't jump when he cut me. I hoped I wouldn't bloody jump as I was supposed to be numb! I shouldn't feel any of it, so why would I jump?

The nurse asked me where I went on holiday the previous year. I wished she would shut the fuck up. *Stop talking to me and stop asking stupid bloody questions.* I managed to say, 'I don't want to talk to you – I just want to lie here and concentrate on my breathing,' to which she responded, 'talking to me will help with your breathing.'

Did she really just say that? She was really winding me up now. WTF did she know? She had never met me and certainly didn't know what would help me. I knew what I had to do to get through the procedure. *Please just shut up,* I say in my head. *Let me just concentrate and do it my way. You are making me feel worse, not helping me, this is not how I cope with things.*

I might have been struggling to speak but, by God, if my arm were not behind my head, and the other clasped in her sweaty hand, I would have punched her straight in the mouth. This memory still makes me so mad. I really regret not saying something at the time. How dare she make my lovely mum (who had travelled all the way from Spain to hold my hand throughout this scary ordeal) move away so she could take her place?

Medics note: listen and respect your patient's wishes; everyone copes with stress in different ways. Ask your patient what would make them feel more at ease. And don't ask stupid questions just because you don't know what else to say!

The doctor said I would hear a loud click – a bit like the sound a stapler makes. He demonstrated with the equipment and sure enough I heard a loud click. It sounded like a very big stapler! He said he didn't want me to jump when I heard it.

My mum watched as he inserted the biopsy needle into my boob and directed it towards the lump. I kept my eyes tightly shut. I heard the click and he said, 'that's it.'

'Thank God it's over!' I said.

'No,' he replied, 'I meant, that's the first one done. We need to do two more.'

Bloody hell! Why can't doctors make themselves clearer? As he took the second biopsy, the assistant nurse holding my hand waffled on. She was told to press the bandage hard on my boob and apply pressure to stop it from bleeding. The bandage was very large and the fact he wanted pressure applied to stop it bleeding made me think that the cut was worse than it actually was. It hurt more when she pressed on it. She was one strong nurse!

The doctor told me I would get the results back in a few days' time. He would also advise the breast consultant about his findings. That would shock Mr 80% Negative. I wish I'd been a fly on the wall when he told him he'd been wrong. Nursey was still pressing on my boob and smiling inanely. At least her questions had dried up so she had nothing further to say. Thank God for small mercies!

I was introduced to a breast nurse who asked if I had any questions. I was still too stunned to ask anything, and to be fair I didn't know what questions I was supposed to ask. I knew nothing about breast cancer. I had no idea what was going to happen next – this was all new to me. I felt like I had skipped Go on the Monopoly board and missed out a load of steps. It was happening all too fast and I was in shock. The nurse wasn't very warm and as I had no questions, that was the end of that. Great nursing skills – well done!

Still in shock, Mum and I headed to the canteen for

a cup of tea and a chocolate bar as my sugar levels had dropped. I knew this because I felt light-headed, I was shaking and dizzy and felt sick to the pit of my stomach. I was crying again, which I think was the shock, though it could have been the fight or flight symptoms which comes in three parts, all of which I had experienced in just one morning:

1. The alarm reaction stage (tick)
2. The resistance stage (tick)
3. The exhaustion stage (tick)

I was now on stage three and absolutely worn out. I phoned Jed to let him know what had happened. He was cross with himself for not coming.

Jed's Story:

Carolann phoned and told me she'd had a positive scan and a biopsy had been performed. I had stayed at home as I was full of the cold and unwell. I think I had man flu but wasn't sure. I was sick to the stomach with worry and guilt for not being there with her. I was so mad with myself; I knew I should have gone with her. I wanted to get in the car and go to her, but she said she was on her way back. I wondered how bad she was, what to say to her ... I sat waiting for her in silence as I couldn't concentrate on anything.

We left the hospital to head home, but I felt so dizzy and light-headed that we had to sit down again on a bench outside the hospital for quite a while. My mum gave me half a chocolate bar to help my sugar levels get back up. (A full bar might have helped me more!)

I was too sore to drive and had been told not to, but my

car was too big for my mum to drive. We hadn't thought of this when we'd told Jed to stay at home. I'd not been expecting to have a procedure carried out.

Getting the car out of its parking space was a struggle but once I'd managed it, Mum took over. I was tired and sore when I got home, and the pain lasted for a few weeks. At one point I rang the hospital to ask if it was normal to still have pain after all this time. Apparently, it was and if the nurse had told me about the after-pain I would have known what to expect.

Results Day

The waiting was unbearable. I checked my phone constantly in case I had missed any calls from the consultant. My phone stayed with me all the time. It felt a bit like when you go to the airport and you keep checking you've got your passport. I had been promised that as soon as the results came through, the consultant would call me. This was probably the worst part of the entire journey: waiting for results. It was either going to go one way or another. A negative result meant I would get my old life back. While a positive result meant I would enter a world of appointments, scans, tests; a whole new scary universe of uncertainty.

Friday 18th November 2011

After another day of constantly checking my phone, the consultant finally called me at 4pm and asked me to attend the hospital at 6.30pm that evening. He said he was driving from Liverpool to see me. Of course, I would be there.

I phoned my mum and asked her to come with me and Jed. I was feeling very positive and upbeat – maybe he was driving all that way in rush hour traffic on a Friday evening to make up for all the blips I had experienced so far. Mum however knew it was not going to be good news. What doctor would drive for over an hour on a Friday to deliver good news? A negative result could have been given over the phone. A face-to-face smacked of something serious. Deep down I knew this but you have to remain positive.

We arrived early at the hospital and sat in the waiting room once again. Both Jed and my mum were very quiet. Their silence was eerie in fact, and I tried to stay upbeat for them, even though secretly I felt sick to the pit of my stomach.

The consultant came into the waiting area and greeted us at 6.30pm on the dot. Well done. There's nothing worse than being kept waiting, especially for results as serious as these. I didn't like the sad look in his eyes and when I shook his hand he just said, 'Thanks for coming.'

I asked how he was and he struggled with the answer. And there you go. That tiny pause was enough to arouse my suspicion. I now knew the appointment was not going to end well.

He took a seat at his desk. I sat in front of him with my mum next to me and Jed next to her. All three of us sat in a row like condemned prisoners. We were all in this together, the three Musketeers.

The specialist wasted no time delivering his verdict as he handed out the sentence: 'I'm so sorry, we were wrong. Your tests show that you do have a malignant carcinoma.'

My eyes were fixed on his as I very calmly said, 'OK. So, what do we do about it?'

I looked at my mum and Jed, who had his head in his hands and looked like he was about to cry. I heard him say, 'Shit.' My mum held my hand and took over with the questions. I recall hearing the word 'cancer'. My mum asked, 'So what do we do next?' and the consultant gave us two options:

1. I could have a mastectomy with reconstructive surgery and chemotherapy.
2. I could have a lumpectomy with chemotherapy and radio therapy.

Mum asked him what he would do if I were his daughter. I think he was uncomfortable with the question but he drew a diagram to explain it to us, which really helped, and then he said, 'I think a mastectomy would be the safest option. That is what I would want if it were my daughter'.

I had no hesitation and agreed with the decision. After all, he was the expert. He told me to go away and think about it for seven days, but I told him very firmly, 'No, I'm a nurse and I know what I want. I don't need time to think about it. I want this decision to be made now and I want this cancer out of me.'

I have no idea why I mentioned being a nurse! My decision was based on the strong positive person I am, along with his advice of this being the best way of surviving it. The decision was made and now we just had to get on with it. There was nothing else to think about and no time to waste letting this bugger inside me grow any bigger than it already had. I wanted whatever gave me the best chance of survival, regardless of what I had to go through.

As a nurse, I also knew this was going to be one of the most difficult journeys of my life. But at that precise moment I knew what had to be done and, as strange as it may seem, I actually felt quite strong.

We left the room and all three of us walked very quietly and subdued through the waiting room of people, down the busy noisy corridors and out into the car park. Mum and Jed got into the car but I stayed outside. I needed to phone my best friend Kimberley. When she answered her phone I just said, 'It's positive, I have cancer'.

It was a freezing cold November night and the bitter wind bit deep into my bones making me shiver as I waited for her response. I felt my coat wrapped around me trying to fight the cold. But the line remained silent and I wondered if she had heard me.

'Are you there?' I asked and eventually, after what seemed like ages, she responded: 'What did you say?'

I repeated my words and it was clear she was in shock. After a brief conversation she told me she would come straight to my house. She had to drive from Wigan and even though I told her it was too far to travel on such a night, she said she didn't care; she just wanted to be with me.

Kimberley had just applied fake-tan before she set off for mine and by God, did she stink! That smell is so distinctive and it still reminds me of that night, even after all those years.

Jed

I'm sat in the car with Carolann's mum. Carolann is outside on her phone. I have my head in my hands and say, 'I can't believe it.' I'm having trouble not crying. Mum puts her hand on my shoulder and says, 'Don't worry – we'll get through it, whatever it takes.' We sit quietly, watching Carolann outside. How must she be feeling? I am numb and as it's unknown territory, I can't guess or even think what comes next. Our world has just been blown apart.

It had taken just half an hour for my life to be turned completely upside down, for serious decisions to be made and for life as I knew it to be changed forever. And now it was all confirmed: my dream had come true. The dream had been my warning that I had cancer. Without it, I would never have checked my breasts and I would not be here today to tell my story.

It transpired I had a grade two, changing into a grade three breast cancer and it had been growing inside me for six to twelve months – the same length of time I had been having my strange, recurring dreams and seeing the black shadow man. These dreams were the scariest dreams I'd ever had, but I cannot thank the spirits enough for bringing the cancer to my attention. At the age of forty-two I was too young to die, and I am so lucky and thankful that the spirits guided me in the right direction. Their guidance saved my life.

We drove home in silence. None of us knew what to say. We were all trying to digest this new information in our own way, wondering what impact it would have on all our lives. I called my daughter Jenna and told her it wasn't good news. I then had to phone my son Ryan, who was studying in London. He needed to know. He was upset and crying, and I felt so bad for him as he was so far away. I just wanted to hug and comfort him. My daughter lived across the road from me so I would be able to give her a hug and discuss things with her. We had each other at this strange and difficult time. I urged my son to go to his flat mate and talk to her about it; she could give him a hug. But it was her birthday and she had friends' round, so my poor son was crying alone in his room with no one to comfort him, which made me feel guilty for telling him. At times like this, we all need our family.

When I arrived home, my lovely daughter was waiting for me. We hugged and she said it would be OK. We were both trying to be strong for each other. Jed put the kettle on to make tea for everyone (it's what the British do best in any situation), and Kimberley arrived. I was sitting on the sofa and everyone else sat around watching me. Most of the conversation consisted of: 'I don't believe it.' I was still stunned and just sat in disbelief. The situation felt surreal. I felt as though I were asleep and when I woke it would have been just another one of my bad dreams. Kimberley gave me a special positivity necklace to wear called a Q link. I had to touch it and keep positive throughout the ordeal.

Kimberley

Deep down I think both my husband and I knew you were going to get told you had cancer, but I tried to stay positive for you. When you rang me on the Friday night, after being told it was cancer I couldn't even speak. I was totally shocked and gutted. I knew I had to come and see you (even though I had just fake-tanned!) I knew we would get through it and nothing was going to change that.

Another Shock Result

Life went on as normally as could be expected for the next couple of days, considering what we had on our minds. As friends and family heard of our devastating news, flowers and cards began to arrive. It all felt so surreal as I was feeling fit and healthy and no different to how I'd felt the week before. I looked and felt exactly the same, and yet I had get-well cards and people telling me to get well soon. This situation was bizarre; I had to start preparing myself to be unwell but I didn't want to be unwell. I didn't have time for this. I couldn't believe I was walking around with cancer in my body. How did I get it? I was healthy and fit and I looked after myself, I just couldn't understand it.

I was also still thinking about my dream. The hospital in my dream was not the private hospital I had attended. What did it mean? That there was another road for me to go down and visit the hospital from my dream? Or simply that my dream was just not one hundred per cent accurate? I mean, it had been pretty accurate so far. It had saved my life in fact, which is just incredible.. I was just so glad that I'd listened to both my dream and my gut and pursued getting a scan when all other forms of tests, and consultations had told me I was clear of cancer.

I paid a visit to my GP, just so I could update him on everything and see about having my care transferred to the NHS. It was another option and would save us a lot of money, especially as I didn't have private health insurance. I sat in the waiting room wearing sunglasses as I couldn't stop crying. I thought my sunglasses would hide this fact but the tears, snot and noise told a totally different story. What the other patients must have thought of me I can't imagine, but I was upset and my body had to do what it had to do. So, I just sat and cried and blew my nose and let my shoulders heave up and down. As soon as I opened my mouth to speak to the GP, both my mum and I broke down again. What was wrong with me? This crying was becoming as regular as my breathing!

I told the GP I had chosen to go private only to get the tests and results. I'd been hoping the tests would be negative and that would have been the end of it. I hadn't thought beyond that, and never in a million years did I think I would get stuck in the private sector. I wanted my operation at my local hospital, so asked my GP if he could arrange for this to be done. He told me if I wanted to have the operation on the NHS, I would have to start the referral process all over again. This would take a couple of weeks, which meant any surgery would have to be after Christmas.

This was devastating news but he said that the private sector would already have had their multidisciplinary meeting (one where all the team providing my care meet to discuss the plan), and therefore I should stay with the private sector if I wanted my operation carried out before Christmas.

He told me that as all my notes and results were with my private consultant, getting them would not be easy. Furthermore, each consultant likes to carry out their own tests and consultations and therefore the whole process would need to begin from scratch anyway. In short, I was best staying where I was.

I felt sure this wasn't right. Couldn't they just request the notes? But I was so upset, and I had no energy to argue with him. I didn't feel my GP was much support with the matter. All I wanted was the opportunity to have the operation on the NHS and at a hospital close to my home, without having to pay over £10,000 (which was just the starting cost) to have it done privately. And this new private hospital was over an hour's drive from my home. But there was nothing more my GP could do apparently, so we were facing a hefty bill. Happy bloody Christmas!

Monday 21st November 2011

The consultant had promised to call me as soon as possible to arrange the operation. I had been expecting to have it carried out at the same hospital I'd had all the tests and consultations at, however, when he phoned me to let me know that he'd booked my operation, he also advised me I'd be having the surgery at the hospital where he practised full time —not the one where he'd seen me previously. He said he'd spoken to the anaesthetist and it was all arranged, but the only date he could get his whole team together was Sunday 4th December – just eight days away! There was no hanging around with him; it was full steam ahead!

He said it would be a package deal and, with everything included, the cost would be £10,000. I didn't have that sort of money but I knew somehow, we would all pull together as a family and find it. I needed the operation and now it was all planned, I just wanted to get it over and done with.

Looking back, I think the consultant must have assumed I had private health insurance, but as I keep saying, I didn't. He told me I would have my own side room with bathroom and a personal nurse for 24-hours, all of which sounded quite nice. I liked the fact that I have my own private room and wouldn't have to share a toilet, especially as it was costing £10,000! However, this 'package deal' turned out to be more costly than originally quoted. A number of extras we were eventually charged, which bumped the cost a fair bit. Thank God for credit cards and the Bank of Mum and Dad!

The consultant asked me to come to the hospital as he needed to discuss the operation in more detail. I wasn't looking forward to it; ignorance is bliss, as they say. The less I knew, the better I felt – he didn't have to explain it all to me.

When Jed and I arrived, we were taken straight into his consulting room. He told me he wanted to show us some photographs of previous mastectomy operations he had carried out but I put my head straight down and looked at the floor; I didn't want to see these photos but he told me I had to look at them. I really didn't want to, as I knew looking at them would scare the hell out of me and make the situation more real. But he would not take no for an answer.

The photos shocked me to the core. Why was he showing me them? I felt that same knot tighten in my stomach, and once again I felt sick. I couldn't speak a word. I was choked up and knew any attempt to speak would result in me crying. And I was trying so hard to be strong and brave, even though I didn't feel strong or brave at all.

I felt so sorry for these women with their battle scars and flat chests. They were real photos of real women who had all suffered the same awful ordeal that life had thrown them. But they had all survived. They had made it through their diagnosis, their surgery, and their recovery. They would all have their own wonderful stories to tell. I couldn't see their faces, but I knew they were standing proud, showing off their battle scars for other women like me who would follow in their footsteps. I wondered where they were now. Had they survived, or had cancer come back and reclaimed them? I hoped not. It took every ounce of my strength to remain strong and not break down. Seeing those photographs made the whole situation suddenly become very real, and I was so scared to become one of them. I was sad for the women and I was scared for what I was about to go through.

My consultant told me I had to stay positive. He said the only way to get through it all was by thinking positively. If I didn't remain positive, I wouldn't survive. According to him, the women he'd treated had survived because they had all been positive. I wondered if I told a man I was cutting his testicles off but urged him to stay positive, would he remain calm or tell me to fuck off?

Then the consultant said, 'When you stand and face the sun, your shadows are always behind you.'

This was a saying that would stay with us all forever; in fact, my son even had it tattooed on his ribs!

A couple of days later the consultant rang to let me know my results were back from the biopsy. Things worked very differently from the NHS. The NHS would have sent me a letter with an appointment, and I'd have had to attend the hospital for these results. Whereas I had my consultant's number saved in my phone so I could contact him at any time, and he could contact me. It was much easier and saved so much time.

Anyway, I hadn't been expecting any more results so wasn't sure what this was all about. I thought they'd done the biopsy, found it was cancer and that was that. But apparently, they had to find out what type of cancer it was so they could give me the right treatment, including which concoction of chemotherapy I was to receive. Every day I was learning more about the disease, just like Sister P had told me in my dream. He told me I had a triple negative cancer, which meant nothing to me. But apparently, if it's triple negative, you don't need to go on Tamoxifen. Again, I had no clue as to what he was talking about. He may as well have been talking in a foreign language. He tended to have these conversations with me as if I understood what he was talking about. It was as if he saw me as a nurse, not a patient, and therefore thought he didn't have to explain anything to me. But I wasn't trained in this area, so had no clue as to what he meant. He'd lost me at triple negative, and what the hell is Tamoxifen?

A quick Google search later revealed that triple negative

cancers are more aggressive, (shit, that's not good) and aren't treated with hormone therapy (which is where the Tamoxifen comes in). Tamoxifen is a tablet taken to slow or stop the growth of the tumour. Women are put on it if they have a hormone-positive cancer which feeds off their oestrogen. The Tamoxifen attaches itself to the hormone receptor blocking the oestrogen. (Clever.)

I also learnt from Google that triple negative cancers occur in only 10–20% of diagnosed breast cancers, and are more likely to affect young people, African-Americans, Hispanics and/or those carrying the BRACA 1 gene mutation. So, I had an aggressive cancer that was prone to spreading and they nearly missed it all together! I'll say it again: thank God I pushed for that scan!

Over the next few days, I hardly ate a thing. I felt so sick all the time. I was desperate to get my old life back. You cannot imagine the feelings a diagnosis like this creates, unless you've been through it: one minute you're happily enjoying life, then suddenly your whole world is turned upside down, like the flick of a switch. The results were a shock to me and although I still didn't fully understand exactly what they meant, I knew the results weren't good. The nurses had warned me not to Google anything, but I say, thank God for Google – it was the only place I was getting my information from. And as a nurse I needed to know everything … apart from what would happen in surgery!

Tuesday 22nd November 2011
The Final Piece of the Puzzle
I was due to have my pre-op. I had been given the address

of the hospital where I was to have my operation carried out, and I would meet my personal nurse for the first time and have all the pre-op tests done there. It took us about an hour and a half to drive to the hospital and as we got closer, I felt that funny feeling in the pit of my stomach again. It felt like déjà vu. Although unfamiliar with the hospital, I felt at ease. I wrapped my coat tighter around me and felt myself withdraw into it, seeking some form of comfort.

We walked very slowly into the hospital and I felt like a prisoner about to face impending doom. I had my hands tucked deep into my coat, my collar pulled high to keep out the draught, and my Ugg boots, which were like slippers, on to keep me warm. We entered the waiting room and BANG: a flashback. OMG! My stomach twisted and I felt a rush of nausea. This was a place I had visited before – not in person though, only in my dream. We sat on a two-seater sofa facing the wall, just like in my dream and I was trying desperately not to cry. I had never ever been to this hospital and yet I *knew* I had been here in my dream – the dream that saved my life! I had goose pimples all over my body and I cuddled up closer to Jed. He had his arm around me, just like sister P in my dream.

'Are you OK?' he asked and I responded quietly: 'I know the layout of this hospital.'

As we sat in the waiting room I glanced at my surroundings: the waiting area was only small, as was the rest of the hospital. It was very exclusive with just a couple of corridors leading down to private rooms and the theatre. There were a couple of doors leading to consultation rooms but apart from the reception area, that was it. It didn't feel like a hospital at all, which helped. It was quiet and calm and just felt … different. You could help yourself to hot drinks free of charge though I wasn't able to enjoy this hospitality – my stomach was too nervous.

I knew I had visited this waiting room before and sat on this very couch facing the same wall, only in my dream. I even knew the corridor I would be wheeled down on the way to theatre. It was all very frightening knowing I had experienced all of this in a dream, and here I was following in those footsteps. How was that even possible? I had no explanation, but the dream had started this journey and everything I'd dreamt, down to the smallest of details, was becoming a reality. And now I was afraid, very afraid, as this also meant that the only aspects that had not yet come true were the two different outcomes from surgery, and one of those had led to my death.

A nurse came and introduced herself. Her name was Sandy (not her real name) and she would be the nurse who'd look after me for the first twelve hours of my operation, and be my nurse for the duration of my stay. This sounded good – continuity in care. She looked so kind and as she approached me for a hug, I put my hand up in defence:

'Don't hug me and don't be too nice as I'll cry. I'm very fragile at the moment.'

I didn't want sympathy; I just wanted to remain strong, the way I have always been, (although I didn't feel very strong at that moment).

Sandy took all my details: name, address, age, allergies, past medical history and explained everything about my upcoming operation. Then she asked if I would like to talk to another patient who had recently had the same surgery. They could phone me for additional support. I told her I would have to think about it and let her know.

Nurse Sandy said I had to have some blood tests and she asked me to get on the bed, which I was grateful for – I didn't want to faint on her! She was aware I was a nurse and said she felt quite nervous knowing this. That didn't fill me with confidence! She placed the tourniquet on my arm but not quite tight enough. Just tight enough for it to hurt as I waited for her to get ready. When she wandered off to get the bottles and forms, I loosened the tourniquet. You should always be prepared. Never keep your patient waiting, whilst you rummage around for bottles, needles, and the relevant paperwork. And never tighten your tourniquet until you're ready to carry out the procedure! By failing to prepare, you are preparing to fail.

I worked as a phlebotomist (someone who takes blood) for many years, and I have to say I was very good at my job – I could get blood from a stone –so this lack of organisation didn't fill me with confidence.

When she eventually returned with the bottles and needle, she didn't realise the tourniquet was now loose, so my veins were no longer bulging out of my arm. I had to pull it tight for her then she struggled to get a vein. Now, I have great veins so there really is no excuse for not finding them. They were practically shouting out to her: 'Here we are! Come and get us!' She could have been blindfolded and still hit the vein! In fact, it would have been harder for her to miss! So, I guided her to the best one and told her not to look so worried.

She said, 'It's knowing you're a nurse that makes me so nervous.'

I was tempted to reply, 'It's knowing you're not great

at your job that's making me nervous!' But when you have a nurse with a shaky hand coming at you with a sharp needle, it's not the best time!

She stuck the needle into my vein and ouch! She went all the way through it so no blood came out. In one side and out of the other! (A vein is a bit like a straw; if you put a needle in and it comes out the other side, no blood will go into it. It would however leave me with a nice bruise).

Her hand was shaking and she said, 'I'm so sorry – I've missed the vein.'

'No,' I replied. 'You haven't missed it – you've gone in too far and come out of the other side! Draw back a little with the needle.'

She did as instructed and to both our reliefs the blood began to flow. When she had bled me enough, she took the needle out but left the tourniquet still tight on my arm. Again, in case you didn't know, never leave the tourniquet on after removing the needle. In fact, remove it before you withdraw the needle. Leaving it on allows the blood to continue to be pushed out.

Sure enough, as soon as she withdrew the needle it started to bleed, and I had to release the tourniquet and take it off. (Am I the patient here or the nurse?) She left me with a nice bruise – just one of many I was to endure over the next few months.

Sandy then showed us around part of the hospital so we would feel more at ease and be familiar with it, which was nice. She showed us where the patient bedrooms were situated, but she didn't show us the corridor that led down to the theatre. Maybe they don't want to scare you. But because of my dream, I already felt I knew the layout; it all felt familiar.

I told Sandy about my dream and how worried I was about the last part – the two endings. I told her what the outcome had been for the two patients and she said, 'Well you're not going to die so stop worrying.' But I was worried, and I knew I had to tell my healthcare team about my worries so they could take extra care of me. They needed to watch my pressures (I have very low blood pressure) and ensure I didn't have a fit, like in my dream. Nurse Sandy was intrigued and asked me lots of questions about the dream. She wanted to know how I'd been positioned on the bed, as there was a specific way they would position me after surgery. When I described what I had seen, she looked amazed but I don't think she quite believed it as, when I told her I felt familiar with the hospital's layout even before she had shown us around, she said, 'You must have visited this place before.' In the politest way possible I said, 'No, I've just told you, I have never been here before. I didn't even know this hospital existed. It's not near my home – it's over one-and-a-half-hour's drive away. I don't have private health insurance so how and why would I have been here? And no, I have never visited anyone in this hospital.'

I gave up trying to convince people. I know what I dreamt, Jed knew what I had dreamt, and I knew how I was feeling as I stood in this strangely familiar hospital, scared shitless.

I had never been in a private hospital until this journey began, and I'd assumed the first hospital where I had the tests was to be the hospital in which I would have my surgery. This had made my dream seem patchy and inaccurate. But now I was here, everything had come together. It felt like the final piece of the puzzle. The dream had been a warning and I had heeded that warning. I had also been shown two pathways: I could choose either to stay positive and fight this battle (the second chance I had been given in the dream), or I could choose to give up and die (the scenario shown to me by the first patient in the dream). I knew which road I was taking. Perhaps the first patient who had died in my dream had done so because I had no experience or knowledge of breast cancer. I had been scared and out of my depth, I'd panicked and let them die. It was only after Sister P told me to learn about cancer to ensure that the second patient survived that my knowledge on the subject had come about. I was still no expert, but I now knew enough about my cancer to ensure I was getting all the right care and treatment. And I would do whatever it took to ensure I survived.

The previous night I had a funny but very real dream about a large round bird. It was bigger than a seagull and it was sitting on my bed watching me. It had a big yellow beak and very menacing eyes. It hopped up the bed towards me, and then stopped and stared. I put my head under the blanket as I was frightened – it was a big bird and to have it so close was unnerving. I peeped over the blanket, hoping it had gone, but it began hopping up the bed again: one, two, three. On the fourth hop, it had landed on my head! I was so scared I put my head back under the blanket, trying to knock the bird off.

The dream had felt so real that once again I wrote it down, just in case. I had no idea what it meant. But I would be slightly worried if a big bird with a yellow beak and menacing eyes were to sit on my head! Can you imagine? And what were the chances of that actually happening?

Thursday 24th November 2011

That evening my lovely friends took me out for a meal. It was the last time I would be seeing them all for a while. I managed to eat, drink and laugh and for a few hours everything felt normal. It was great being back to the old me again. I told them about my cancer dream, which had potentially saved my life, and they were all amazed. None of them had ever experienced anything like it. Then I told them about the dream with the big bird. They all laughed and one of my friends said, 'There's something very weird going on with you if that dream was to ever come true. And realistically, it can't come true – where do you find a large round bird with a yellow beak and menacing eyes that would sit on your head?'

Who knows but let's see if anything ever comes from it. My friend added that if it ever came true, she'd want to see photographic evidence!

Friday 25th November 2011

I woke up feeling quite good. I was starting to lose a bit of weight, and I knew this was down to stress. But hey, any weight loss when you're carrying a few extra pounds has to be good, doesn't it? Silver lining to every cloud. My son was finally coming home from London. It would be so great to see him again and to reassure him about everything. We had not seen each other since my diagnosis, and it would be good for him to see exactly, what was going on. Being with his family might put his mind at ease as so far, all his information had been second hand over the telephone. My lovely daughter had been really good with everything but was carrying the full weight of the burden on her own, so having her brother around to talk to and share her load would hopefully help her. I am so lucky that my children get on well and have each other for comfort.

We were all going out to watch the Christmas lights switch-on in town and some of our dancers were to perform as part of the event. It was a really lovely night out and it gave me another rare chance to feel like life was back to normal again. Also, as part of the entertainment they had a boy pop band who were going to perform after us. We were waiting backstage with them. They were only young lads and were messing about with the other entertainers. I turned to see what was making them all laugh and scream, and was shocked to see that they were messing around with a large stuffed round bird with a big yellow beak and menacing eyes! They were making the bird bob up and down, and then – you guessed it – they sat the bird on my shoulder and shouted, 'selfie!' Just as we were about to have the photograph taken, they sat it on my head for a laugh. I was stunned!

I immediately sent the photo to my friends who I'd been out with the night before. Now they were my proof; all ten of them had heard me describe this dream just twenty-four hours earlier, and now here I was with the bird sat on my head, just like in my dream! They were all as shocked as me. Another strange dream had come true but the meaning of this one was beyond me. To this day, nothing else from that particular dream has come true, but just as the bird was big, bright and clear in my dream, it was just as big and bright in real life.

According to Google, seeing birds in your dreams symbolizes goals, aspirations and hopes, though to dream of birds attacking you suggests you're being pulled into many directions. That sounded a bit like me; I felt I was being pulled in all directions, but I wasn't sure if the bird was jumping on my head to actually attack me or not. Dreaming of colourful birds apparently means you're with the right person. Well yes, that part is definitely true: Jed is the right person for me. And dreaming of a very large bird can indicate something very difficult in your life. Well yes, that was also very true at that time. Birds are messengers from the spiritual realms, it claimed, symbolizing peace, transformation and power. So, a lot of these meanings did relate to me.

Later, when I was having chemotherapy and it got to springtime, I would have the bedroom window wide open as I loved to hear the birds singing outside whilst I was bedridden. Birdsong really cheered me up when I was down and to me, birds also represented the end of my treatment, as I knew once the spring was over and they all went quiet, my treatment would also be over. Even to this day, when I go for a walk a little robin will always appear either in front of me or next to me. On one occasion when we went for a walk, I didn't get to see my little robin and I commented on its absence to Jed. But as we got into the car, it flew down and sat on the fence within touching distance of the car watching us.

Saturday 26th November 2011
The News is Out
This was the day that I let everyone know at the dance school that I had cancer. They had to know as I was going to

be absent for a while, so it was best just to tell them the truth.

Lots of parents hugged me and asked about the operation. I was upbeat and made the story sound funny (I decided it was better than being sad and morbid). I even allowed them to feel the lump. Some of them couldn't feel it even though I placed their fingers exactly on it. Most of the women said they would be scared that they wouldn't know what a lump felt like and that they would be terrified they would miss it. I reassured them: if you can't feel a lump it's probably because you haven't got one! I thought that by allowing them to feel it, I was helping to educate them.

Looking back, I wish I hadn't let them have a feel as all that prodding could have caused a bit to break off and travel somewhere else in my body to spread. I'm not even sure this can happen, can it? Perhaps I'm making this scenario up but that's what I imagined after being told by my consultant that stress may contribute to cancer. He said to imagine a stream of water rippling softly over little stones; the stones are the cells and the water is the blood. When you get stressed, the rippling water starts to travel faster and as it gets faster it gets stronger and disturbs the little stones. One of those stones can then break away and travel somewhere else until it gets stuck, and once it's stuck, more and more stones will pile on top of it until it is large enough to be felt as a lump. Quite a good description I think and so to this day I try not to get stressed – not an easy task but I try!

Everyone at the dance school was interested to hear what my operation would entail and I was more than happy to explain it all to them. I told them they would be cutting my nipple off and I was worried they might put it down and lose it. What if that happened? Then I thought of other body parts they could replace it with – stick the end of a finger on instead! And what if the surgeon walked out of the theatre and there it was: my missing nipple, stuck to the sole of his shoe like a piece of chewing gum!

You had to laugh about it even though it was a serious subject. And they do say laughter is the best medicine as it increases blood flow, improves your heart health, and lowers stress hormones (which I definitely needed to keep under control). Laughter would increase my immune cells and infection-fighting antibodies (which I needed increasing ready for my fight ahead), which would then improve my resistance to disease. So, I needed as much laughter as I could get to help me get through my journey and it was free, (they do say some of the best things in life are free). No matter what I was going through and the bad days yet to come, I found that laughing helped me to forget it all, even just for a few seconds, and I needed this; it helped.

The mums found it easy to ask questions about my cancer and probably asked me more questions than they ordinarily would, knowing that I was very open and happy to discuss it. I felt it was as good a time as any to educate anyone who was happy to listen and interested in learning more about the subject. I was pleasantly surprised at just how many questions I was asked and at how interested these women seemed about this taboo subject. Prior to my diagnosis I knew nothing about breast cancer, and I still had a lot to learn. But if it could happen to me it could happen to anyone. And when do you ever get the chance to sit down and have in-depth conversations like this? Most people kept illnesses like cancer to themselves and would never discuss it in great detail like I did. But I had a platform and women eager to ask questions; being able to educate them was quite liberating. So many women will be unfortunate enough to get this horrible disease and I'd been uneducated about it when I was diagnosed – that was what made it so scary. So, if I could give even a little of my knowledge (that's all I had!) and it helped one other woman, I was happy.

A week later one of the mums asked to speak to me privately. She said she had found a lump in her breast nearly a year ago but was so frightened it might be cancer that she hadn't told anyone, not even her husband. Hearing me dealing with my cancer so positively and openly had encouraged her to visit her GP, and to confide to her husband. Listening to me showed her that cancer was not as scary as she'd first thought. In fact, it was less scary facing it than ignoring it and living in fear. Sure enough, she was also diagnosed with breast cancer. I was glad to know that because I had been so open and positive, I had at least helped one other person. If one person was saved by getting an early diagnosis, then that was good enough for me.

You always get one though, don't you? And this one was one of the mums who had just newly qualified as a nurse and was working on the cancer wards (so she was obviously an expert). She took me to one side and said, 'You should think about this very seriously as this is a massive operation.'

(Thank you for that …)

'The fact you are acting so calmly and joking about it, makes me worried. You must realise the seriousness of it. I work on these wards and I see this operation every day.'

(Well, you've only just qualified so, technically, you're not an expert)

'And you need to understand what you're about to go through.'

Was she for real? Of course I knew what I was about to go through! I was living and breathing the situation on a daily basis. I knew the full impact and seriousness of it, but this was how I had chosen to cope with it. I was also a nurse (though that made no difference to this disease) and it was *my* job to educate those women who wanted to listen to me. So people, if you don't agree with how someone chooses to deal with their illness, then please just mind your own business and let them get on with it in their own way. If you don't have anything nice to say, then don't say anything! It was my illness and if I wanted to deal with it by laughing then I would. I either had to laugh or cry, and I knew which one I preferred. I knew how serious my illness was, but no matter what I had to go through it, I had no other choice, so I may as well laugh my way through it. And I can honestly say that I made it through my illness because I had my wonderful family supporting me, I remained as positive and upbeat as much as I could, and I laughed as much as I cried. Laughing lifted me momentarily out of my horrible situation, just enough to make it liveable.

I have to say though that by the end of that day after all the prodding and probing, my boob was very painful. I had a burning sensation in my neck, and I couldn't lift my right arm up. Every now and again reality would kick in and remind me that what was happening to me was all very real.

Sunday 27th November 2011

All day I had been imagining what I would be doing this time next week. And let me tell you, my imagination was running wild: both boobs chopped off, nipples lost, having a fit, drowning in water. If only I had listened more to my consultant! But with just one week to go I had lots to do in preparation for being ill: I needed new pyjamas and slippers (don't we all need new pyjamas and slippers when we go into hospital, or for Christmas?) If I was going to be ill, I may as well at least look good and be comfortable. And I needed to make sure I was all ready for Christmas, as after this week, there would be no more shopping trips for me for a while. It might be my only chance to actually save up some money, so there's always a bright side!

Friday 2nd December 2011

I was feeling very positive. I had to see my GP for a sick note, which was a first for me. I was sitting in the waiting room when Doctor Nasty walked past. He looked as miserable as ever. I heard the other patients say they call him 'Dr Death'. Wouldn't you think he would at least ask how I was doing or at least acknowledge me? Come on man! Two weeks ago, you thought I had cancer; at least show some form of communication. But no, there was no bedside manner here or, should I say, waiting room manner. Although however nasty and ignorant we all thought he was, he did come good for me in the end – I will give him that. He did his job.

Do you remember Nurse Sandy had asked if I had wanted another patient to call me for support? I'd told her I'd think about it. Well out of the blue, I received a phone call from a lady, wanting to offer me support. In spite of telling Sandy, I'd think about it, she seemed to take this as a yes. And to be honest, I hadn't given it another thought – now here was the lady on the other end of the phone!

What part of 'I'll think about it' did Nurse Sandy not understand? Anyway, I didn't want to appear rude, so I had to accept the support she was offering. After all, she had taken time out of her day to call me. Her support consisted of informing me all about triple negative cancer, which I then had to research again on the Internet, as she told me some new things I hadn't seen the first time.

I don't know about support, but she certainly terrified the life out of me! No one wants to hear about someone else's operation only two days before their own, especially how bad it was and how unwell she felt afterwards! She advised me about drinks I should get in prior to having my chemotherapy and how much that had helped her. (Let me tell you, each person is different and what may have helped her certainly didn't help me. I tried the drinks and tips she gave to me but nope, none of them worked!) Anyway, two days before my operation, all I wanted to hear was positive news delivered with a smile from a friendly person, not doom and gloom. I wish I hadn't spoken to her now and in hindsight (and if we're comparing) I think my recovery from surgery was even worse than hers!

Note to self and others. Never Google your illness!

Saturday 3rd December 2011
Today is the Day!
Following a long day at the dance school, which really helped to keep my mind occupied, and for which I was

grateful, by 6pm reality had well and truly sunk in. I felt sick and nervous knowing that my operation was the following day.

Jed had gone to see my mum; he knew when I needed time alone. My stomach was in knots again and I felt like it was doing somersaults. I felt like I was struggling to breathe. I was so anxious, my chest felt tight, and I felt numb to the core. I just wanted to curl up and go to sleep. I was suddenly cold, and so so tired and as I climbed onto my couch, my coat wrapped tightly around me, I curled up in the foetal position, and then the tears came. Not just little tears but great big fat droplets running down my face. I didn't even feel the need to wipe them away. I just let my body do what it had to do. I had no energy left, I had stayed strong all this time and I needed this release. I just wanted to cry and feel some sort of relief. I needed to feel sorry for myself, if only for five minutes. In this safe, quiet, private space of my own, lying in the dark, I felt like I just wanted to fall asleep and not wake up until this nightmare was all over. This all felt like a bad dream and I wanted someone to wake me up and tell me it had all gone away. But for now, I just needed to be on my own so I could lose control and not have to be strong for everyone around me. I didn't want sympathy and cuddles; I just needed this time to cry and be alone with my thoughts for a while. Who is this person I have become? It was not like me at all. I am normally such a strong, positive person and can cope with all the pressures life usually throws at me. That night, I was just a blubbering wreck.

But just as I was getting into the flow of this crying lark, (it's taken a lot of practice and I still can't do it in public or in front of my family) my mobile rang. It was Kimberley. She told me not to be a miserable bitch and to pull myself together. She told me to stop milking the situation; we all have problems (this was our private saying and it always made us laugh). She had a way with words as you can tell – there would be no sympathy here! It was time to pull myself together. The moping was doing me no good. Kimberley was right and I loved her for caring. She has always been there for me whenever I had needed her. Her timing (phoning me in my hour of need) was perfect, which was strange. I never ever wanted to feel that low again. I took my comfort coat off and my Ugg boots (I was wearing my Uggs a lot) and I began the task of showering, shaving, fake tanning and painting my nails in preparation for going into hospital. You've got to look good no matter what the situation; the show must go on!

Mum
Jed arrived at my house and told me Carolann was upset and lying alone in the house. I wanted to go to her but I knew she wanted to be alone, which is why she had sent Jed to my house. I sent Kimberley a text saying just three words: "HELP MY GIRL."

Kimberley
I received a text message from Carolann's mum asking me to help her daughter. I phoned Carolann straight away and it was clear she was upset. I would soon sort this out!

Ah, so that was why Kimberley's timing had been so perfect! Mum had told her to call me. Now it all becomes clear!

Sunday 4th December 2011

The day had arrived: the day I lose one boob and gain a new one. So, the procedure I was having is called a mastectomy, followed by a latissimus dorsi flap which is the reconstruction part of the surgery. I am having both procedures done at the same time. Following my mastectomy, an incision will be made near my shoulder blade and an oval shape section of skin, fat, blood vessels and muscle will be slid through a tunnel under my arm skin into my breast which, along with an implant, will create a breast shape. The blood vessels of the muscle will be left attached to the original blood supply in my back. How exciting! Not quite the bionic women but as close as I'm ever going to get!

In spite of knowing all this, I did manage to sleep a bit the night before. I woke a few times but to be honest it was more the smell of the fake tan keeping me awake – I stank! You know that fake tan smell? I couldn't wait to get up and have a shower to wash the residue away. That is the only problem with tanning this way: you have to go through the stench before you come out the other side looking great. The end result would be worth it though and by 4.45am I was in the shower getting myself ready as if preparing for a special day out (I wish).

My phone beeped and I noticed quite a few of my friends were already up. I read the messages of support they had sent, which was really nice. I wasn't allowed a cup of tea, so Jed chose to drink his downstairs – he didn't want to drink it in front of me, which was so thoughtful. I felt calm with no worries or problems at that moment. I was just going through the motions. It all had to be done for me to survive, so I had no other choice than to go along with what had been planned for me today.

We drove in relative silence for over an hour and a half to get to the hospital and as soon as we began to approach it, I started to become nervous. This was so scary; I was going into hospital feeling really well. I was fit and healthy, (apart from the cancerous lump growing inside me) and knowing I was about to lose a part of me, filled me with absolute dread. The fear of the unknown was playing havoc with my insides. My stomach was churning so much I was convinced I would vomit and pass out. They say that nerves and excitement are the same feeling and normally I would agree, but that day I couldn't. I'd never been so scared in my life. How your body can keep functioning, when every body part and cell scream out and rebel in fear was beyond me! Nothing in my body felt like it was working as it should. Everything was saying turn and run, but I had to ignore the feelings and use all my willpower to stay focused. This was one of the biggest challenges of my life. To turn and run was the coward's way out and that would have led in no doubt to my death. Anyway, if it had been my time to die, the spirits would not have forewarned me in my dream. They had helped me, shown me a glimpse of the future. Now I had to stay strong and positive and help myself.

My mum had wanted to go to the hospital with me, but I had asked her not to come. Not because I didn't want her there, but because I didn't want her to see me going through all of this. I was trying to protect her. In hindsight I wish I *had* asked her to come as, just then, I really needed my mum. But it was too late, and besides I didn't want to cause her any more stress. I would just have to get on with it without her. I had also told my family that no one should visit me for the first couple of days, as I would just be asleep. Again, I was just trying to protect everyone. Honestly, I wanted them all with me, but I didn't want to cause them any worry or stress by seeing me hooked up to all the equipment. It was a stupid thing to say really as nothing would ever have stopped my daughter or my mum from visiting. And in fact, they would be even more worried at home wondering what was going on.

Looking back now, I wish I had asked my mum to be with me, but I didn't want to make a fuss or put her through any more of the ordeal than necessary. I'm sure she wanted to be with me and I still feel the guilt of this now. Mums are stronger than we give them credit for. Sometimes we need to just step back and let others look after us. I just didn't want to lose control and become a patient. Poor mum must have been frantic at home. Why did I always have to try and be strong and brave?

We parked in the hospital car park and I watched as Jed got out. When I knew he wasn't looking, I left a card on the driver's seat for him to read when I was asleep during the operation. This had been a hard task to achieve, as he'd been so busy, fussing over me and watching my every move. I had also left a card for both my mum and my daughter. I had posted them through their doors early that morning with special messages written from my heart, just in case I didn't make it through my operation. I know: very negative, but I wanted them all to know how much I loved them … just in case. There was always a risk with any surgery, and I wanted to make sure they all knew just how much I loved them if anything did go wrong.

A healthcare assistant showed us to my room. She explained how to work the TV and what to do in the event of a fire. The room was quite nice and resembled one in a Premier Inn. Except in a few hours' times it would be turned into a recovery room with me attached to all sorts machines, drips, drains and bags. Kimberley arrived on time for the first time ever! Her and Jed were brought tea on a tray (which I was not allowed) and then the countdown began.

07.30am – Bloods taken, urine sample taken, gown on back to front, ready for the marking of my boob.

08.40am – The consultant came to see me and marked my skin with a black pen, showing roughly where he would make his incisions. He drew big arrows and markings (which only he would have understood the significance of) on both my front and my back. And he marked the boob on the side on which he was to operate, (to make sure they removed the correct boob in theatre!) Argh! I was so scared! This was the first time I had seen him in his theatre scrubs and seeing him dressed ready to operate on me made my stomach flip upside down. This was all so real now. I was *sooooo* scared!

08.45am – The anaesthetist came to see me and informed me I was now not going down to theatre till 10am. We had originally been told 9am. All this waiting was making me worse. I didn't think it was possible to become any more nervous than I was already, but as time ticked on, I did. I became more nervous than I ever thought possible. I lay on the bed trying to concentrate on my breathing, but nothing helped. I had gone past the point of no return and nothing was going to calm my nerves. I was exhausted and just wanted to sleep. My friends had all said that at 9am (when we'd all thought I'd be in theatre) that they would watch the DVD *Bridesmaids* whilst I slept. It was something they could all do together and it was such a funny film that it would give them all a laugh. The delay in going to theatre scuppered those plans. *And* my mum would have had time to get there to be with me. Damn! If only I'd known!

09.00am – Recovery Nurse came to see me. Another conversation I didn't want to have!

09.42am – Still waiting. Argh!

10.07am – Finally they came for me! Nurse Sandy just said, 'It's time.' I was so scared. I had to walk down to theatre. And here was the next part of my dream! The corridor we walked down to get to the theatre was the same corridor I had walked down in my dream! I thought I was going to have a panic attack. I told Sandy I had been here before. She said, 'You must have been shown around when you came for your pre op.'

I told her I hadn't been shown around this area. In fact, it was her who had showed me around so she should know they don't show this part of the hospital to patients on induction. I had never been in this hospital apart from my pre-op and again today. And today was my first time in this corridor apart from in my dream. She *had* to listen to me. I felt as if I were talking but no words were actually coming out. Why wasn't she taking any notice of what I was trying to tell her?

I was now very scared as I remembered the two different outcomes in my dream. This was the final part of my dream and everything so far had come true, so walking down this corridor to the theatre was very disconcerting. This was one of the final details from my dream and now all that was left was the outcome of my surgery. It could only go one way or the other and I prayed for a positive outcome, God help me! Jed had also walked with us to the doors of the anaesthetic room and after saying our goodbyes, he left to go to the Trafford Centre to do some Christmas shopping, pass the time and keep his mind occupied. I just hoped I got to see him again.

Before we went into the anaesthetic room I tried once more to convince the nurse that the next part of my dream was playing out. But it all fell on deaf ears and she just said, 'You will not die, stop worrying.' She was so blasé. I looked back at the corridor we had just walked down and clearly remembered walking down it in my dream. I had just let my first patient die and Sister P had seen me and asked why I was crying. She had then sent me into another room to try again with another patient with a tumour. This corridor was that same corridor from my dream. I took one last glance down the familiar corridor as I reluctantly walked into the anaesthetic room, like a doomed man walking to Death Row.

Jed had made me a playlist to listen to and I had this playing. The first part was relaxation music: Feng Shui – all new to me, and then the rest were songs we both liked and were meaningful to us. I closed my eyes as we entered the anaesthetic room because at that same moment, the anaesthetist came out of theatre, so I got to see straight into the operating theatre, something I didn't want to see. It was too scary to think about what was going to happen and I certainly didn't want to see the room in which it was all to take place.

The nurse asked me to lie on the bed. OMG this was it! I was shivering; I was so cold so they let me keep my socks on. I was shaking with nerves and felt like I was in a really bad dream. I wish I had been! I felt like I was going through the motions and it wasn't actually happening to me; it all seemed fuzzy and unreal. They put these strange, blow-up legwarmers on my feet to keep me warm and I was lying there waiting for the inevitable when they informed me there had been a delay in theatre – something to do with the patient in front of me, so I would have to wait a little bit longer. Bloody hell! How much more waiting? I was seriously shitting myself here. Every time we got one step closer, two more steps appeared. It was like running in a dream and getting nowhere! I wasn't sure how much more my heart could actually take. The theatre nurse took my left hand in hers and her hands were freezing (what's new?) I wish she could have warmed them up – I was cold enough already! I didn't want to speak though; I just wanted to lie listening to my music and concentrate on breathing as normally as I could. My heart was racing but I needed to keep calm. I was just too scared to make small talk. I felt sick with apprehension and wanted this nightmare to be over. I needed to relax and go to sleep. She gave me this space, something for which I was grateful. She just rubbed my hand and told me it would be OK. She understood what I was trying to do. I liked this nurse for her understanding. I was now looking forward to being put asleep. At least I would have a few hours of peace and tranquillity. Nurses, please warm your hands up!

I lay very still with my eyes shut tight so I couldn't see

what was going on around me. There seemed to be a lot of people in this small room, and I didn't want to see what they were all doing. I listened to my music whilst they inserted a cannula in the back of my hand. I was singing along quietly. Well, I thought I was quiet, then I noticed the staff were laughing. I hadn't realised how loud I was actually singing as I had my earphones in! The anaesthetist said it was the first time he had ever had Meat Loaf in his theatre. I was singing along to *Two Out of Three Ain't Bad* and moving my feet in time to the music. I loved this song and as I was singing away, Nurse Sandy, who was holding my right hand, was making jokes about my choice of music. The music changed from one song to another as I waited patiently to go into theatre. Thank God Jed had made me an extensive playlist!

Then, the anaesthetist nudged me to get my attention, just as I was in full flow and said, 'Right, it's time for you to go to sleep.'

Ooh shit – this is it! The rollercoaster was at the height of the climb and I felt like I was about to go over the top with no safety harness on. I was so scared! I reminded them all that if I had a fit, I would die, as this was what had happened in my dream. I begged them to please really look after me and watch my pressures just in case. They said, 'You're not going to die,' and as they put the cold liquid into my cannula, I immediately felt the effects as it started to travel up the vein in my arm, into my blood stream. As this happened, I couldn't believe that the song that had started playing was mine and Jed's special song: *You're Beautiful* by James Blunt. The song had a lot of significance for us, and I told them to wait till we got to the chorus before they put me to sleep. I asked Sandy to tell Jed that I was falling asleep to our song and she assured me she would (she didn't though). I also asked her to fill in some of my diary of the time spent in the room (but she didn't).

I could feel the liquid sleeping potion as it travelled into my system just as James Blunt sang, 'You're beautiful, it's true.' Then I fell asleep. Those words meant so much to me and Jed, yet if they had taken me in on time, I wouldn't have heard this song play as it was quite a way down the playlist. You could not have written this chapter any more perfectly than it actually happened!

Jed

I walked with Carolann to the anaesthetic room. It was like walking the Green Mile. I thought they would let me stay with her till she went asleep, but they just told me to say goodbye and took her in. She was very scared again as she had recognised the corridor from her dream. I walked back to the room, which was now Carolann's, and Kimberley was still there. We both just looked at each other and she said, "It will be OK, Carolann will be fine." We hugged and both left. As I got into my car, I noticed a card lying on the seat. I opened the card and read it. I started crying. The words Carolann had written in the card made it sound like she wasn't going to come back. I then realised for the first time that this could actually happen. She had written the words:

Whilst you read this I will be sleeping, and I cannot wait till I awake and see you again. If my heart beats, I will always love you.

There are many words in this card but even to this day I am unable to say them without breaking down. I have been unable even to this day to read this card through without crying and giving up. I don't think I will ever get to the end.

I rang Carolann's mum and told her she had gone into theatre. I went to the Trafford Centre to try and pass some time. They had told us she would be up to four hours in theatre. I walked into a jeweller's shop to buy some earrings, and when they asked who it was for, I told them it was a Christmas present for my partner, but she might not make it as she was having an operation for cancer. I started to get upset again. The girl was shocked, and she asked if I wanted to sit down. I sat down for a minute but then I left the shop and just stood watching everyone moving about in the Trafford Centre. I felt like my time had stopped whilst everyone else's was moving around me. This is a memory I get each time I see the TV ads for cancer. I had to get back to the hospital. I couldn't concentrate. I needed to be near her.

I had only been about two hours and when I arrived back at the hospital, I stood looking at the empty room. The consultant then arrived in his theatre clothes and said everything had gone ok. I asked him why it had only taken a couple of hours and he said, 'Why take four hours, when you can do it in two and a half?'

He then shook my hand and said she would be back soon. I was asked to wait in the relatives' room for five minutes by Nurse Sandy so they could set the room up and get Carolann back. I waited for what seemed like ages. Half-an-hour had passed and still no sign of Carolann. I was then advised that she was having a bad time coming around in the recovery room. She had had her maximum dose of morphine and she was still in pain and not coping well. About ten minutes later I saw them wheel her past. I had been warned about all the equipment that would be around her, but what I saw shocked me to the core. It looked really bad. She had drips, an oxygen mask, tubes coming out of her back, catheter bag, and tubes blowing warm air onto her. She was conscious. I could only kiss her forehead as this was the only area I could get to. Nurse Sandy was checking her breast every 15 minutes to make sure there was sufficient blood flow to the nipple. She told me to look at the new boob. I didn't want to as I was scared it would look like one of the pictures, we had been shown a couple of weeks before. Nurse Sandy said, 'You need to look.' I was so shocked when I saw the results. Even though it still looked black and blue with bruising, the reconstruction was amazing.

Carolann's daughter and her mum came up to see her. It was hard to understand what Carolann was saying as she was so drugged up. We gave her sips of water with a straw through the hole in the oxygen mask as she wasn't allowed to take it off. I couldn't leave her that night and stayed by her side all night. The nurses gave me a mattress and I slept on the floor next to her bed.

I woke up in the recovery room! Wow this was a weird situation. I couldn't even remember going to sleep and now here I was awake, and it was all done and thank God I was alive! I had survived – I was so relieved!

I think I was also in pain, so I asked the nurse for more pain relief. I wasn't sure if it was pain or just a natural request for me to ask for pain relief. I had always preached to my family and friends that you don't have to endure pain and that you should always keep on top of it, and that is what I had planned to do. I told the nurse I was not a 'mardy' so if I say I have pain it's because I do. She told me I'd already had the maximum dose of morphine and so she would have to speak to the consultant.

I looked over to the opposite side of the recovery

room as they had just brought another patient back from theatre. She was a lady, possibly in her mid-60s. She was still intubated (had the breathing tube in her throat). She was confused and tried to sit up. The nurses immediately looked after her. They told her she was OK and to give a little cough so they could remove the breathing tube from her mouth. I watched as they removed this and she lay back down as they placed an oxygen mask on her. It didn't faze me watching this as I have worked in theatre before, however I think it could have been scary for a patient who wasn't used to these surroundings and maybe this is something they should have taken into consideration. There was only one theatre so it was a case of one patient in and one patient out ... so how long had I been in recovery if this lady had managed to have her operation and was now also here with me? I was very confused!

My consultant was then by my side and talking to me, but to be honest I don't recall the conversation as I was still very sleepy with all the medication in my system. I recall something to do with my low blood pressure (something I always suffer from) – I'd told them to watch my pressures! I was watching his lips as he spoke to me, but for all the money in the world I could not understand or make out what he was talking about.

They put something into my cannula and I fell asleep again. At some point during the next week he would come to me and say, 'Do you remember me telling you about it when you were in recovery?' and I would respond with 'NOPE.' Why do consultants try and speak to you after surgery when you're still out of it? It is a bit like the dentist asking you questions when they have their hand in your mouth!

As I was wheeled back to my room down the familiar corridor from my dream, I saw Jed waiting for me. The team had prepared my room with all the drip stands and made room for all the equipment I was attached to. I was in room 408. I don't recall much for the rest of the day. I was very sleepy and would wake every now and then and see Jed, my mum, and my daughter. I would try and speak but they couldn't understand what I was saying, and it was so frustrating to me as I knew what I wanted: I was very thirsty. I had an oxygen mask on, and I had to sip water with a straw through the gap in the oxygen mask. I wasn't allowed to remove the mask even to have a drink. I felt the blood pressure cuff pumping tight every fifteen minutes and I was aware of Sandy checking my breast every fifteen minutes. She asked me if I had looked at my breast and I said, 'No.' She said I needed to look at it. I was scared but when I looked down it just looked like a normal breast except there were some bruising. I was still too out of it to take it all in but so far so good. I didn't look any different. I still had my boob and my nipple so there was nothing to be frightened about. I found myself hoping that part wasn't a dream!

Mum
Sunday night
I was under strict instructions not to visit Carolann on the day she had her surgery. However, we received a late change of heart by my lovely daughter saying she didn't mind us coming to visit. Jenna had already said there was no way she was not going to visit after the surgery. She needed to see for herself that her mum was OK and being well cared for. We set off at 4pm and after using

three motorways, M60, M56 and M6 we arrived at the hospital at 5.20pm. The room Carolann was in was very dimly lit and the heat was overwhelming. It had to be kept at a high temperature to help keep her warm and therefore ensure a good blood flow, which is needed to preserve the nipple. The noise of the equipment clicking, and whirling was daunting. Carolann looked very white. She had no colour at all in her little face. She had a Bair Hugger covering her up, which is a type of blanket that pumps warm air around you. This was heaving up and down. I could see a blood stain on it. I didn't like this at all, but I held my tongue (not easy for me). Jenna went straight over to her mum. Carolann saw me standing in the doorway and said, 'It's alright come in.' It was a relief that she was quite with it – better than I had expected her to be. Even though she was connected to drips, drains, leg flowtrons, Bair Hugger, a catheter, and had an oxygen mask on, she still tried to reassure us all that she was doing OK. The Bair Hugger was up to her neck to protect her new boob, but she popped her little hand out of the side of the bed for me to hold, which I did, and this was my main role for Sunday and Monday. Neither Jenna nor I wanted to leave the hospital that Sunday evening, not because it was raining heavily which then turned to sleet and snow, but because she looked so poorly and helpless. It was hard walking away but an overwhelming relief that we knew they had taken out the dread lump. Jed was great and we knew he would look after her until we returned the following morning. He did too! He stayed with her all through the night. Thanks Jed.

Sunday Night

I watched as Jed fell asleep on the chair next to my bed. I told him to go home but he said he was too tired to drive the long journey home and the weather was really awful. The night nurse brought him in a fold-up bed so he could stay with me. They told him he had to be up early so they could put the bed away before the day staff saw it. They would normally charge for relatives sleeping over. How mad is that? Jed slept all night in a deep sleep. The last couple of weeks had taken a toll on him. I tried to look over at him, but I was in too much pain to move and I realised that even if I wanted to, I couldn't actually move myself. Realisation hit me! I was stuck semi-upright, slightly on my side (just like in my dream) in the bed and I could not move my right arm. I would need the help of the nurses if I wanted to move myself in the bed. They had not warned me about this, and it is was quite scary not being able to manoeuvre yourself, and to be reliant on the nursing staff. Ooh how the tide had changed! Jed slept very quietly, and you would never have known he was even there. He slept through all the hustle and bustle as the nurses stepped over him to do my observations, blood pressure and check my breast. The nurse was trying to get into my wardrobe to get my toothbrush but struggled as Jed's mattress was in the way. She wouldn't move him though as she didn't want to disturb him.

I had slipped down the bed and the night staff struggled to move me back up. They eventually put a blue sliding blanket underneath me and kind of slid me up the bed. It was a real struggle for us all and I couldn't assist; I felt helpless. Was I really that heavy? I think it was because Jed was under their feet asleep, and they couldn't get into a suitable position to move me easily. They had the cot sides still up on the bed and really, they should have put these down to manoeuvre me, as they had to stretch up and over them. They continued to struggle with the cot sides still up which made moving and handling much harder for us all and wouldn't be kind on their backs. Also, Jed was in the way, which meant they could not get to me from one side. I told them to wake him, but they didn't want to disturb him, which was thoughtful to him but not so good for me or them!

I remember, as the nurses were changing me, they both looked down as if they were looking at my private parts. Then they looked at each other, as if to say, 'What is *that*?' They never told me what they were looking at and, still being very woozy I said nothing. It did make me think perhaps I'd had an accident, or something had gone wrong, and it concerned me the way they looked at each other. I never found out what they were looking at and I was not aware of having pooed myself … and I had a catheter in so I couldn't have wet myself; only they will ever know. But I will always remember that look between them, and even though I was woozy, it still made me feel very uncomfortable.

Tips for nurses: Please do not exchange a look and then not speak. Just because we are patients doesn't mean we're not human and or unaware of what's happening around us. It bothered and worried me then, and as much as I was out of it, I was still aware of that strange look you shared when looking at my private bits!

Monday 5th December

Jed had left for work early to ensure he didn't incur a charge for sleeping over. I woke as I heard the distinctive rattle of the breakfast trolley. I wondered what breakfast would be. I was quite hungry and looking forward to it but no one came to me. I wasn't offered any food or even a drink. After a couple of hours, I realised I'd been forgotten about entirely.

The hours passed and I drifted in and out of sleep. At the time I thought maybe I wasn't allowed to have breakfast due to the operation but I should have known better, being a nurse. I know you must eat in fact, and this was day two. However, due to the medication I was taking (morphine), I was drifting in and out of sleep and I wasn't thinking straight. I tried to reach my nurse call button but I couldn't– they'd left it attached to the wall. I shouted meekly 'Hello!' but no one answered my call. (Maybe they couldn't hear me with the oxygen mask on). So, I went back to sleep. I was hungry and thirsty and needed a nurse, but I was unable to move or reach the call button. I was stuck and feeling very vulnerable. I would have laughed if I'd had the energy. I could hear the nurses going about their daily tasks, but no one came to see me. This was a private hospital and I was paying for this service! Nurse Sandy had been with me for the first 12 hours but had now gone home. I felt so alone and helpless. Nurses: make sure your patient's call button is always within reach for them.

Finally, a nurse came into my room and I asked her if I was allowed to eat and drink. She said, 'Of course you can eat and drink! Have you not had your breakfast?'

When I explained that no one had come in to offer me any she was shocked and ordered me some scrambled egg and tea. This was now quite late in the morning. She said, 'You have to feed your boob.'

This phrase was subsequently used a lot during my stay in hospital. Well I would feed my bloody boob and myself if you brought me some food to do so!

At long last, a tray of food and tea was brought to me by the catering staff (in private hospitals nurses don't get involved with the catering). However, they just quickly placed the food down on my table and left before I had the chance to say I needed help. Wouldn't you think the catering staff would have had some sort of training so they know to make sure the patient can reach the food? And if not (and they can't help) surely, they could let a member of the nursing team know?

I tried to sit up, but I couldn't. I tried to move my arm a little, but no, it just lay there like a dead weight. No one had warned me this was going to happen. This was so frustrating! I looked at my right hand and urged it to move but again, nothing. I had no control over it. It just lay there next to me. I tried to see if I had psychic powers: I stared at it and imagined it working but nope, nothing. I tried to reach out to pull the food closer to me but it was too far away, just out of my reach. Bugger!

I looked for the nurse call button but it was nowhere to be found. I couldn't see it on the wall so it must have fallen behind the bed. Wherever it was, it was out of my reach so I drifted back to sleep, still having not eaten. When I woke up much later, the uneaten food had been taken away. The catering staff must have come in whilst I was asleep, seen the untouched tray and assumed I wasn't hungry.

The nurses came and washed me but I don't really remember much of this time. They then made the decision to remove my morphine button as I was having too many hits. Not sure how that works – it's set so you can't overdose – but apparently, I was at my limit and my blood pressure was dropping very low. They said not to have any more for a few hours. I don't even remember pressing it, unless I subconsciously thought it was the nurse call button! I then began with a headache, which was to become the worst headache ever. And no, I *still* hadn't eaten. I don't remember any of this in my dream!

Mum

Poor Carolann: first they forgot to give her breakfast, then when they do it's put so far away from her, she is unable to reach it. Then she couldn't call for help as her nurse call bell was too far away. She has now started with a headache. Her room was so hot and we weren't allowed to open the windows, as she had to stay at a certain temperature. We made sure she always had her nurse call button next to her. They were washing Carolann so we waited in the day room. There was a nice student nurse on duty; she is very considerate. Her name is Sarah and she brought us tea in the day room.

Mum and Jenna had come to visit me. I was very uncomfortable but couldn't sort myself out. Once again, I had slid down the bed and been unable to do anything about it. My oxygen mask was rubbing my face and making it red and sore. I tried to ask them to help me, but they couldn't understand my instructions; they thought I was just mumbling. In my head I was clearly asking for help and it sounded like I was talking normally to them. It was so frustrating not being understood. I desperately needed to be in a better position – I was too vulnerable. You know when you watch those horror films when someone is tied up and trying to escape? And you're urging them to hurry up as the perpetrator is on their way back, but they are being too slow, and you shout at the TV and it gets so frustrating? Well, that's how I felt right then. I would have had no chance of escaping if my perpetrator was on his way back. I would have just given up! They had prepared me for my surgery, but no one had prepared me for what I went through afterwards or what I was to endure over the next 48hrs …

Mum
We decided to go and get some food and a coffee. We were told we could walk to the hospital next door, which is an NHS hospital, as

they had a WRVS. It was run by three women, each with different learning difficulties. One woman was very angry and mumbling obscenities, one woman looked like she had anorexia, and the third woman was much older and was looking to have a row with someone – anyone. She was very angry. She found an unsuspecting gentleman (who had dared to ask for a drop of cold water in his black coffee) and instead of just giving it to him, she wanted to know why he needed it. She shouted at him saying it was black coffee – why did he want cold water in it? And no, you can't have cold water – you asked for black coffee – putting water in it would make it cold. The gentleman knew there was no hope of getting cold water so just accepted his coffee and walked away. Then it was our turn. You can imagine we were a bit uneasy as to what would be said to us when we ordered. So, we asked, not ordered, if we could please have a cheese and ham toastie to take out. This request made all three of them go into full panic mode! They were not happy about us taking it out; why couldn't we just sit in? But they made the toastie anyway. However, when it arrived, we couldn't find any cheese in it. It contained a tiny piece of ham with the smallest amount of cheese stuck to the back of the ham. And it wasn't quite toasted (and it was dry) but it was food and after a bit more commotion, we left and went back to see Carolann. We thought it best not to complain, they were doing their best.

Tuesday 6th December 2011
One of the worst days of my life!

My headache was extremely bad and was making me feel really sick. I had struggled all night with it and had asked the nurse for some pain relief but she hadn't come back to me. The day nurses hardly ever came into my room.

Because my room was next to the nurse's station, I

could hear them all talking. They really should be more careful as I could hear all their conversations. They clearly didn't realise how loudly they were talking, and the conversations they had were not professional ones!

I saw the young student nurse, Sarah, and I told her my headache was getting worse. I felt sick and I was sweating; I was soaked with perspiration. I asked her to ask her colleagues if there was anything I could have for the pain. I heard her tell the nurse at the nurses' station (who was obviously fed up hearing about it) and I heard the reply:

'I know she has a headache; she keeps telling us. What does she want us to do about it? We've given her everything we can – she can't have anything else.'

Again, no one came into my room to check on me or even to explain there was nothing else they could do for me. I still couldn't get up or move myself in bed and I felt so sick. My head felt like it was going to explode, and every little noise was like a bomb going off in my head. I was so hot and uncomfortable, and I felt that the nurses were just not bothered. If I hadn't been so unwell, I would have been really angry and sorted it out. I was in a private hospital following major surgery and I had been left to my own devices. Private or NHS, they are all still nurses with the same training behind them and they should have been looking after me.

It occurred to me that I was learning so much being a patient and I wasn't enjoying the experience! If they'd known I was going to write about them, maybe their approach would have been different. My head was off the scale with pain and I had no energy to speak. It was a nightmare!

My mum, Jenna and Kimberley all arrived to visit me.

We were all sitting in the dark and I couldn't speak to them, I felt so unwell. I could hear my mum reading a magazine and every time she turned the page it was like a knife cutting into my head. They were all whispering but the noise was incredible. They may as well have been shouting at the tops of their voices as every little sound they made was magnified, tenfold. But I couldn't tell them to be quiet as I couldn't speak, I felt too sick. The effort to even open my mouth was just too much. I flinched at every little sound. I just hoped that if I lay very still and didn't move or speak, it would help with the pounding headache and nausea. Kimberley left after about an hour and then Jenna had to go and collect her children. Poor Mum sat in the dark with me, bless her. When Jed arrived, he saw us in the dark and thought we were asleep, so he went and sat in the day room until we woke up! Eventually Jed realised we weren't asleep and came and sat with me, which meant my mum could go home. My family liked someone to be with me during the day so that my care was not compromised.

I was delving even deeper into the darkest and worst hours of my life (or so it felt at the time). I lay in the dark with the worst headache ever, feeling so sick I couldn't move an inch. The headache was causing me more pain and discomfort than the surgery had. All my horrible symptoms were due to this headache. I couldn't have the lights on and the sickness meant I couldn't eat or drink.

Sandy (who was off that day) had kept telling me I must eat, but I just couldn't. I had no appetite and I knew if anything went into my stomach, I'd be sick. My head was pounding so much I actually thought it would explode. Surely no one could have this sort of pressure in their head and something not rupture? None of the nursing staff realised how ill I was and not one of them had taken the time to find out.

Meals were placed in front of me and taken away uneaten. Observations were taken and the staff continued with their main duties (but not caring – their most important duty). Jed didn't know what to do and I couldn't speak to tell him, I was so unwell. I felt if I could have died there and then, I would have. I know: very powerful words, but that shows just how unwell and how low I felt at that time. WHY WERE THE NURSES NOT LISTENING TO ME? I needed my daughter or my mum to come back and help me. I knew my daughter couldn't come – she had the children. So, I told Jed to ring Mum and ask her to come back to the hospital. Of course, my darling mum said she would come straight away. After more than an hour's drive home, she got straight back in the car and drove to get back to me. A mother's love is endless.

Although Nurse Sandy was off, she had given me her phone number in case I needed her. I was so emotional; I had to call and tell her how bad I was feeling. I just couldn't cope anymore, and I didn't know what to do. She said she would call in and see me. This was really nice as it was her day off.

When she arrived, she hugged me and told me it was natural to feel weepy a few days after an operation. She changed my oxygen mask to nasal specs (the ones that sit under your nose), as my skin was red and sore from the mask. My nose had also started to bleed and was sore from the high volume of continuous oxygen I was having. My temperature was up to 38.2 and my blood pressure 60/50. I felt really ill. Everything was painful, and my drain sites and boob hurt. My urine was a yucky lime-green colour, which they said was normal. I was so low and could not stop crying. I even told Jed to go home; I didn't want anyone to see me this low.

Although Sandy had explained about post-op depression, I just could not pull myself together. I was very ill, and this continued for the next twenty-four hours. I couldn't even think about food, although everyone repeatedly told me I had to feed my new boob to save my nipple. I was brought scrambled eggs. I couldn't even pick the fork up as it was too heavy, and the egg kept falling off it. I had no strength and ended up eating a few mouthfuls using my fingers like a child. What the hell was happening to me? Eating with my fingers! I was now in survival mode and knew I had to get strong and gain back my independence. I was so not prepared for all of this: the operation itself had been easy, but this recovery with the headache and all its symptoms, along with the lack of basic care, was something else.

I felt guilty bringing my mum back to the hospital; it was such a long way to come. I didn't know what else to do though. Emotionally I was starting to settle down, but my headache and sickness were at a level that meant something had to be done before my head exploded. And once again I needed my mum to be my voice.

Then it came to me: I realised this was not a normal headache but the worst migraine ever. Why had no one thought of this? Why hadn't I thought of this? I'm a bloody nurse and know the symptoms of a migraine. I could not believe it hadn't occurred to me before now. Bloody hell, what a relief! I may know the answer to get rid of this headache. I asked the nurse if they had anything for a migraine. They said they didn't stock anything for migraines, but there was a Tesco up the road and Jed could go and get something from there. I felt all my Christmases had come at once when he arrived back with migraine tablets and I took two straight away. Within the hour, I started to get some relief. Never mind morphine, Migraleve is the answer, and choice of drug for today. Thank you, Pfizer, for making this drug!

My consultant came to see me in the afternoon and said, 'You have to get up.' I told him I couldn't get up – I felt too sick to move. The next thing I knew he took me by the arm and said, 'Come on – sit up, it will make you feel better.'

As he helped me up, I said, 'I'm going to be sick if I get up.'

'You're not going to be sick,' he replied.

But I could feel something lying heavy on my stomach and the minute I started to move I felt it swish and my stomach started to heave. I told him again I was going to be sick, and again he contradicted me. He sat me up on the edge of the bed and then made me slowly move to a chair. I was up no more than thirty seconds when I felt so sick and dizzy, I tried to get back onto the bed but before I knew it, I vomited all over the freshly made bed. I looked at him and said, 'I told you I was going to be sick,' as he very quickly left the room. You haven't got cancer, oh you have, you won't be sick, oh you will. I know my body – just listen to me!

I have to say though, I felt so much better for being sick and getting rid of whatever had been lying on my stomach. Having relief from the migraine and no longer feeling sick meant I could start to recover properly, and I intended to recover as quickly as possible so I could get out of that hospital!

Mum

I sat with Carolann today in the dark. She was having a really bad day. I sat with a magazine and every time I turned the page she flinched. Her head must have hurt so much. I just wished I could have taken all the pain away from her. The hostesses were very nice today; they were called Mary and Mark. They had been very nice with us bringing us tea and checking we were OK. They brought Carolann cottage pie, but she couldn't eat it, so I ate it rather than waste it. I wish I could get her to eat something. All her meals are being eaten by me or Jed. Carolann told Jenna she wanted to die today, which showed how poorly she was feeling. She said that the nurses didn't seem to want to help. If she hadn't realised that she had a migraine and asked for the correct medication, then no one would have known and then how long would she have had to suffer? But it is not down to Carolann to think as a nurse at present. She is a patient needing care, but once again she has had to use her own judgement as no nursing staff had bothered to speak to her, find out what her symptoms are or help and support her. This headache could have been resolved a lot sooner if they had!

Wednesday 7th December 2011

Mum

I sent Carolann a text at 7am. She said her headache had finally gone and she no longer felt sick. She said she was feeling much better. Thank God. I am so relieved.

Light at The End of The Tunnel

Yeah, I felt like a kid on Christmas day. I had woken up with no headache and the sickly feeling had gone. I felt so much better. Why don't hospitals stock migraine-relief medication? I could have got on top of mine a lot quicker if they had realised it was a migraine and if they stocked the right medication to help. If they had only bothered to ask me about my symptoms, they would have realised what was up with me two days previously! If I hadn't been so unwell maybe I would have realised it was a migraine but I was the patient here; it shouldn't be down to me to diagnose what's wrong! Pity my dreams couldn't have helped with this one ...

I was due to have my catheter out – another step closer to recovery. I didn't mind having a catheter *in situ*, as it was good not having to worry about getting up to go to the toilet, (how lazy was this?) Not that I could have got up anyway, but as soon as this catheter was removed, I would have to get myself to the toilet. I was nervous about having it removed as again, this was all alien to me, and I was unsure of what to expect.

The nurse came and took it out, which was actually OK. There was no pain or discomfort so that was a relief, but then she just left the room. As soon as the catheter was removed, I felt as if I was starting to wee myself. I needed a commode as I would never have made it to the bathroom in time. My mum asked the nurse to bring me one but as usual our request was ignored. I was still unable to get to the bathroom unassisted and I was panicking I was going to wet myself. My daughter went to get help. She asked the nurses sitting around the nurses' station, explaining I needed it urgently. None of the nursing staff got up to fetch one and not one of them came to help me, so once again, I was left relying on my mum and my daughter to get me to the bathroom. I was very wobbly on my feet and Jenna was furious that no one had come to our aid. The nursing care was appalling! Maybe I wouldn't have wet myself; perhaps it was just a feeling because the catheter had been removed, but the nurse could have explained that to me if it was the case. I didn't know what to expect – this was all new to me. I had never had a catheter in before.

The physiotherapist also came to see me. She showed me how to 'rock the baby' – an exercise to help strengthen my arm. It was an effort just to lift my right arm and I could only do it by supporting it with my left hand. I rocked my arms as if I were rocking a baby and although I could do ten of these, it was such hard work. I don't remember ever being told this would happen to my arm, and it was quite alarming discovering that my arm was literally paralysed following surgery. The physio supported me walking to the day room and back, which was a great effort but also a great achievement for me. I had to hold my drains and bags in a carrier bag. I was so tired walking just this short distance, but I soon managed to do this little walk four times a day. Every day I was getting that little bit stronger.

I could also now get to the bathroom with some support to have a wash, and I even managed to eat some soup. Look at me go! I had walked into this hospital an able adult and within twelve hours I had become reliant on others for my basic needs, and I was reduced to feeding myself with my fingers! What had happened to me?

Another of my consultant's patients came to see me. She was ahead of me with her treatment and showed me her breasts; this is something breast surgery patients do. They are often quite happy to show and compare their breasts. I have to say they looked really good. It is so clever what this consultant can do. She was wearing a wig as she had lost her hair following chemotherapy and she asked if I wanted to see her without the wig. I told her I wasn't ready for that yet. The thought of losing my hair was the one thing that I was dreading. No, I didn't think I was going to lose my hair. I did not like the idea, so therefore I am not entertaining it. There had to be a way to combat this from happening. I would have a think about it and maybe do some Googling but for now, I will not discuss it. No, no, no! I didn't mind looking at her breasts, but I didn't want to see her bald head!

Feeling mischievous

I sat in my room listening to the day staff rattling on. It was better than the programmes on television. I heard them complaining that the night staff didn't do anything. How wrong they were! The night staff worked really hard. They said there were jobs still left to do, but they couldn't be bothered doing them. Another nurse said, 'It's nearly time to go home so let's just leave them for the night staff. We'll just tell them we've been too busy to do all the jobs today.'

They were all in agreement, saying the night staff were lazy. I couldn't believe what I was hearing. There were only two night staff on each night, and they had to look after all the patients on the ward. The night shift was just as busy as the day shift. I had watched them passing my room, back and forth; they never stopped and were busy all night long. They always made time to check in on me though and this was their time to sit down for five minutes. One night, following a little chat, one of them said to me, 'We must get on with our work as we don't like to leave jobs for the day staff – we know how busy they are.'

Bless them! They were so nice. If only they knew! The day staff had left me, forgotten to feed me, and forgotten to change my bedding (they stripped my bed one morning and never came back to remake it. Mum and Jenna had to make it up for me at teatime).

Later that evening, I wandered slowly into the kitchen where the night staff were and noticed they were making hot drinks for patients. I asked if I could have one. They said, 'Of course you can. Did you not give your drink order to the day staff?'

I didn't have a clue what they were talking about. Apparently, the day staff were supposed to ask all patients if they would like a night-time drink. This order was then passed onto the night staff. I had not had a single late-night drink since I had been in hospital. Yet again, I'd been missed out. The night nurse made me a lovely Horlicks, which I thoroughly enjoyed. The night staff were so lovely with me and I really enjoyed the little chats we had. They knew I was a nurse and always made sure I was well looked after during their shift. If only they knew how rude the day staff were about them!

Thursday 8th December 2011

My consultant came to see me. I asked whether he knew if the cancer had spread and if so, would the chemotherapy get rid of it? I also asked him if he thought I was going to die! I still don't know a lot about this illness, but I was learning fast. He reassured me I was not going to die, which is always nice to hear from a consultant, though he had been wrong before, so who knows … let's not dwell on that anymore. Everything that had happened to me so far had happened really quickly. From the dream I'd had just two weeks previously, to where I was now: in hospital with my mastectomy and reconstruction completed – it was just crazy. But after a week of being in hospital, I just wanted to get home and the following day might be the day of my release. To get back to sleeping in my own bed and regain some sort of normality would be amazing. Little did I know that life was never going to be my normal again!

I wished I had my appetite back so I could eat some of the lovely food in the hospital. It was like something you would order in a five-star restaurant and I had missed out on so many lovely meals and desserts. The desserts were amazing! You should have seen the size of the banana split they brought me. But I would look at all the lovely food delivered for breakfast, lunch, and dinner, then watch as Jed devoured it. God damn my appetite! I had always had a great appetite, yet here it was letting me down when I really needed it. It would have been a great week to be spoilt rotten but no, I still didn't have an appetite. All I had was my consultant telling me I must eat to feed the boob. I should have had this mantra tattooed on my body!

Yet again, no one bothered to take my late-night drinks order. But now that I could walk on my own (and knew the nurses should have taken my order) I decided to go and find them. It was all very quiet on the ward but I found a couple of the day staff congregating in the kitchen area.

'Can I please order a drink for tonight?' I asked politely.

The nurse looked at me blankly and said, 'We didn't know you wanted one.'

Was she for real? You wouldn't bloody know I wanted one unless you came to my room and bloody asked! *It's not bloody rocket science!* (I wanted to shout, but didn't). It wasn't like me to remain calm and say nothing when I was blatantly being ignored but I felt so vulnerable. I was unable to do much for myself and I thought if I peeved the nurses by making a fuss, they might ignore me even more. Maybe they weren't ignoring me; perhaps they were just incompetent, who knows? Anyway, I said, 'Yes, I do want one. No one has asked if I wanted one, which I why I'm asking you now.'

I must have been getting a bit better as I began to feel the need to occupy my mind. It was time for a little bit of fun ... with a little bit of revenge on the day nurses thrown in! That night, the night nurses (who had been run off their feet) were telling me how busy they were. They were desperately trying to get all their jobs done so they didn't have to leave them for the day staff. After all, they knew how busy the day staff were and they didn't want to add yet more jobs for them to do on top of everything else.

You guessed it: after the crap treatment I had received from the day staff, I thought it was the perfect time to share the not-so-nice conversation I had overheard. I told them the day staff had called them lazy and deliberately left jobs for them to do. (Hey – that's what they said; I'm only saying what I heard!) I also mentioned that according to the day staff, the night staff didn't have anything to do – why should *they* have to do all the work when they could just leave the jobs for the night staff. Needless to say, they were not best pleased to hear this but they needed to know. Revenge was sweet!

Up to this point, the day staff (excluding Nurse Sandy) had forgotten me on several occasions. They had forgotten to order my breakfast, not bothered to get me a commode, forgot to make my bed after stripping it, spoken rudely about me when I had a terrible headache, not provided the basic standard of nursing care I would have expected, failed to take my night-time drink order, not checked on me or left the call bell where I could reach it, and spoken rudely about the night staff, who *did* actually look after me. This was all very basic nursing care and they couldn't even manage that! I told the night staff that the day staff had also said the night staff didn't have anything to do, and all they did was sit about all night, so they had more time than them to get the jobs done. They were furious with these comments. They said I should apply for the manager's vacancy at the hospital, so I could sort the day staff out! If only I could, but the hospital was too far away from home. And God help them if I did because I would not allow this standard of nursing care on my ward! But for now, I would just be mischievous and entertain myself. Whatever gets you through the day, hey? I just hoped that the night nurses left a few jobs for the lazy day staff to do, instead of running themselves ragged!

I felt like a mystery diner checking out a restaurant, which, let me tell you would have received a terrible review. But this was a hospital, a private hospital, which I was *paying* to be treated and cared in, and the care was certainly not up to scratch. I once covered a shift in a private hospital, and was told the patients pay for their treatment so to make sure they were given everything they want – don't give them anything to complain about. But nurses, regardless of where they work, whether in the NHS or the private sector, should always treat their patients the same – as if they were their own family. It doesn't matter if the patient is paying for their treatment, the care should always be the same. The private part is based on the facilities: the en-suite room, the food, and the speed that you get an appointment in the first instance. You don't pay for different standards of care or treatment from nurses or doctors just because they work in the private sector; you expect the care to be the same. When you sign up to be a nurse, you sign up to look after *all* patients regardless of their financial status. I didn't receive even the basic of care on some days and this was just not good enough. I should have complained but at the time, when you are so low and unwell, you put up with it. Then you go home, recover and forget all about it. But if we don't speak up or complain when something isn't right, then the next patient and the one after and so on, will all receive the same poor standard of care, and the cycle will never be broken.

My Beautiful Gran

At 6.45am I text my mum to let her know I was awake and
had taken all my medication, but I was feeling really sickly
again. She said she would be with me soon. I began dozing
on and off, waking up with little starts. Whilst I was dozing,
I felt my left hand, which was under the cover, being held.
I kept my eyes closed for a little longer as I was very relaxed
and happy that my mum was with me. I knew it was my
mum as she had been holding this hand whenever she had
been at the hospital. Mum has lovely hands; they are small,
soft, warm and smooth. It was really soothing and I was
so glad she was with me. I opened my eyes to look at
my beautiful mum, but to my surprise she wasn't there. I
looked around to see where she was but there was no one
in my room. So, who had just held my hand? This was so
bizarre. I definitely felt someone holding it. I even looked

at my hand in case I could see any indents to prove what I had just felt but there was nothing there. I am positive someone held my hand, but I now know that it was not my dear mum as she'd not arrived at the hospital yet. Whoever it was had had to put their hand underneath the blanket to reach my hand. Mum arrived at the hospital at 9.30am. I told her what I had felt and we both agreed it had to have been my grandmother, my mum's mother Jean, who passed away when I was 20. She would have wanted to hold my hand in my mum's absence. How lovely was that?

I was due to have my drains out that morning at about 10am. On cue, Nurse Sandy came into my room to carry out the procedure, something I was really quite scared about. Once again, I had googled the procedure and read many horror stories about drain removal. People say it feels like your insides are being ripped out so I wasn't looking forward to it. Never Google. When will I learn?

I lay on my side as instructed and she told me to take a deep breath. She told me that as I let the breath out, she would remove the drain.

'Ready?' she asked.

'Wait!' I shouted. 'Just repeat that again. Did you say "breathe in and hold it and then when you pull, I breathe out at the same time?"'

'Yes, just follow my instructions,' she said. 'Breathe in.' I did.

'Breathe out. It's done,' she said.

With relief I said, 'That wasn't too bad.'

Then she laughed and said, 'I haven't done it yet!'

I gasped in horror, then she added, 'I'm just messing with you – it's out.'

I was mortified and she laughed saying it was just a little joke. What sort of a nurse thinks it's funny to play a trick like that on someone? I'd been so nervous. What had I done to receive this care from all these nurses? That was so not funny! Sandy however thought it was and left the room laughing, saying, 'It gets them every time!'

Mum

Carolann didn't have a good night. She has a sore throat and her tongue is covered in a white substance. We thought it was thrush, but the doctors say it isn't. I am making her drink plenty of water. She told me about her strange experience when she thought I was holding her hand. I hope it was my mum looking after her in my absence. She had her drains removed this morning. She was so nervous, but it wasn't as bad as she thought it would be. Sandy made a little joke, which I wasn't impressed with – Carolann was nervous enough. She has two blisters: one on the side of the new boob and the other at the wound on her back. Carolann is spotlessly clean as usual and has been up and in the bath on her own this morning, which is an achievement.

I have been to reception to pay some of her bill. Today I paid £3,500 on one credit card, £400 on another and £400 on a third card. I paid £63.00 in cash. We had to pay some of the bill prior to the operation on Carolann's arrival at the hospital. I told the receptionist about the poor service and how, at times, we couldn't get a cup of tea. We were then told there is a visitor's menu, which we could have ordered our meals from. No one had told us this! Why didn't we have everything explained to us in the first place? We had all skipped meals to sit with Carolann whilst she was poorly and would have appreciated a hot drink and something to eat. Apart from sharing what Carolann didn't eat, we hadn't eaten a decent meal since she had been in hospital. We are doing all the last-minute things in preparation for Carolann being discharged today, fingers crossed.

Preparing to go Home

Nurse Sandy asked if she could bring another lady in to see me. This lady also had breast cancer and was due to have the same surgery as me in a few days' time. Of course I would see her. I knew exactly how she must be feeling – only a few days ago I was apprehensive waiting for my surgery. If I could show her how good my boob looked and reassure her that everything would be OK, it might help her to worry less about her upcoming operation.

She came into my room and I show her my surgery site on my back and my new boob. She asked a few questions about how I felt after the surgery and I told her everything had been OK with no problems. I didn't want to tell her about my headache and everything that had gone on because I didn't want to scare her. She told me she had suffered from breast cancer years ago and had to have part of her breast removed then. A mammogram had shown that the cancer had returned. Bloody hell! I didn't want to hear negative stories like this and yet, as I was to find out, most people I met on my journey had suffered from the dreaded disease once before and it had returned to claim their lives. This had reaffirmed my decision to have a mastectomy and reconstruction to get rid of as much breast tissue as possible. And I must admit I looked good! I was so proud of my new boob. This lady would be fine in my consultant's hands. I can't believe the amount of people who had already seen my breasts!

We heard a few days later that my consultant had hurt his leg and was going to be off work until after Christmas. The lady I saw would have to have her operation rescheduled to a later date and with another consultant; I was gutted for her. I had been so lucky. Imagine building yourself up like I did for it all to be cancelled a couple of days before.

At 2.10pm (a very important time in my life) I was sitting with my mum in my room when Nurse Sandy came in and closed the door behind her, which was strange. She never closed the door when she came in to speak to me. She said they had just had the results of the biopsy through and she had asked the consultant if she could tell me the results; she didn't want me to have to wait any longer, and he confirmed she could. I didn't know I was waiting for any results, so I had no idea what she was talking about!

Results:

Tumour size: 12mm

Lymph nodes: clear

Margins: clear for 5mm around surrounding area

Mum

We are so happy! I hug my beautiful daughter and thank God for answering all our prayers. Nurse Sandy hugs Carolann. The relief is overwhelming. We just can't believe that we have been so lucky that the aggressive type of cancer she had didn't get the chance to spread, due to Carolann dreaming about it and acting on it so quickly. Her first visit to the doctors was 11.11.11 and now 09.12.11 she has had her mastectomy, reconstructive surgery and now the news that her lymph nodes are clear. It's just amazing. This has all taken almost exactly one month and it's been a rollercoaster ride for everyone, especially Carolann. She has been so positive and brave, despite being so ill with worry and anxiety.

We rang Jenna and Ryan straight away to give them the good news, and then texted all her friends. Her phone didn't stop bleeping as friends sent messages to her. Jed was so relieved and at 4.30pm he admitted he was really tired. I think his tiredness was down to relief.

Nurse Sandy was hugging me. My mum was hugging me. I didn't really understand the news. Once again nothing had been explained to me, so I wasn't sure what we were celebrating. They were telling me to tell everyone the good news and said I must be feeling so relieved and happy. To be honest, I hadn't even thought about the cancer, the biopsy, or the results. I think everything had happened so quickly that I hadn't had time to figure it all out. I didn't even know they had sent the tumour off for tests so as far as I was aware, I wasn't waiting for results. As naïve as it sounds (especially with me being a nurse), I should know they send all tumours to the lab for testing, but I really hadn't given it a second thought. Until the previous day, when I'd asked my consultant if I would die if the cancer had spread, I had never once had any thoughts about dying. I had never once thought about it spreading. It was there and they removed it and now it was gone. It was never discussed with me what we would do if it had spread, so I had never had any of these thoughts. Each day had just been a battle to get well again following the surgery. In hindsight I was so glad I hadn't had these thoughts, as on top of everything else, I wouldn't have wanted that worry. My naivety was a blessing.

But now I knew what size the tumour was, I was keen to measure it against a ruler or tape measure. We thought it was about ½ inch, so we asked the nurses if they had either a ruler or a tape measure, but no one did. I couldn't believe it could have spread and I could have died. WTF! That is just crazy!

I wasn't allowed to go home till I had the correct sports bra, which we hadn't purchased prior to going into hospital as, again, no one had told me to. With the surgery and swelling and the mastectomy it was going to be hard to judge what size I would need, and now we knew they had no tape measure on the ward, which would have been handy, it was all going to be guess work. Poor Jed had the task of sourcing a bra for my release and he had a terrible time trying to sort the correct size out. The task was like the story of the three bears. We all know it's hard enough for a man to buy underwear for us ladies without having to choose a specific bra and when they don't even know the size! Mind you, most men don't know the correct size when it comes to underwear and just purchase whatever looks red and flimsy. It reminds me of a time when my ex-husband brought me underwear to go home in following the birth of our son: he brought me the smallest pair of G-string knickers he could find and a see through lacey bra, both in red! With my sore, painful breasts engorged with leaking milk, which meant I had to wear breast pads, and my Dr. White sanitary towels (which were huge), there was no way I was going to wear that underwear, let alone fit into it. How was I supposed to balance my Dr. White pad on a G-string? I ended up going home in big Bridget Jones pants, a maternity bra and my slippers, as my feet were as swollen as my breasts and couldn't fit into shoes!

The first bra Jed bought me was too big, and they told him it had to be changed as it wouldn't give me the support I needed. It looked all right to me but who am I to know? So off he toddled back to the shop, (the shop wasn't just around the corner, so these trips took a couple of hours each). The second bra was too small but, luckily, he thought about it and brought a couple of different sized bras with him (smart thinking!) so the third bra fitted well enough to allow me to be able to go home. Well done Jed!

Nurse Sandy suggested I had my tea before going home. This final meal consisted of soup, salmon, carrots, turnips, and buttered cabbage. It sounds delicious but Jed had to help me to eat it yet again. My appetite was still not good, but if I didn't eat, I couldn't go home. Jed and my mum had been helping to eat all my meals since I had been in hospital and yet I still didn't look like I'd lost any weight! The nurses thought I had my appetite back – little did they know!

By now it was 4.45pm and I was tired. The weather

outside was miserable; it was raining heavily, very windy and cold, and the sky was already black as night, but I couldn't wait to get out in it. I just wanted to get home. I was so excited to be going home. *Get me outaaaa here!*

I just had to have my blood pressure, temperature and pulse taken first. The nurses had struggled to get my blood pressure reading. At lunchtime one nurse had four attempts but couldn't get a reading so she changed the machine she was using. It took her a further four goes before she gave up and said she would get another nurse to have a try. It was now 5.20pm and the nursing staff were *still* struggling to get a blood pressure reading from me. Was I ever going to get out of here? Finally, after multiple attempts, a different machine and a couple of different nurses, they managed to get a reading. It was 113/78, which was good so at last I could leave. Though much as I wanted to go home, I was not looking forward to the long car journey in rush-hour traffic on such a miserable night.

Nurse Sandy came with all my medication and a six-week sick note. I was dressed in my jumper, leggings, Ugg boots and comfy coat. It felt strange to be getting dressed in the dark to go home. I was officially discharged at 6.15pm from the hospital.

After been cooped up in a room for a week in temperatures over 30 degrees, stepping outside was a shock and I began to shiver. The weather was so awful – it was so *so* cold. It was raining hard and the wind and rain swept up and wrapped around me like a cold wet blanket. My boob was not impressed with the piercing cold wind and I immediately experienced pain and discomfort through my boob and chest.

The journey home took about one and a half hours and I felt every bump in the road. I held my breast for support as it hurt each time we went over an uneven road surface. It was still raining heavily and there was a lot of traffic on the motorway but I enjoyed seeing the dim lights of the cars passing us by, all busy traveling to wherever they had been: work, Christmas shopping, going out, going home – all doing normal things in life. I couldn't wait for this to all be over so I could get back to my normal life. I felt like a bird that had had its wings clipped; I needed to fly, not be grounded.

I noticed that since going into hospital, people had started preparing for Christmas. It was quite satisfying to see all the Christmas trees in people's windows with the fairy lights twinkling away, lighting the world up on that dark, gloomy night. I had forgotten it was nearly Christmas and seeing how people had decorated their windows for the festive season kept me occupied on the journey home. Life had certainly not stopped whilst I'd been in hospital for a week. I was exhausted by the time we arrived home and went straight to bed. I didn't even drink the Horlicks that Jed made for me. I hadn't even ordered it – he just made it for me. He would have made a good nurse. His kind actions made some of the nurses that had looked after me look bad.

Wow! My own bed at last! I sank into my big mattress with no cot sides and room to spread out. This is what I had been looking forward to. I slept quite well, only waking on a few occasions with an annoying cough. And – oh boy – here was something else to get used to: when I coughed it hurt my boob. The more I coughed, the weirder and sorer it got. Because the boob muscle was still attached to my back, it still thought it was a back muscle. So, when I coughed, I would use certain muscles including this back one. And each time I coughed, my boob would tighten and try to sneak back under my armpit. It was only trying to go around to the back to do the job it was supposed to do. After all, it had been a back muscle for forty-two years and now suddenly it had to become a breast muscle. It was confused and, from the way it was behaving, not very happy or impressed at its new role! This was an extremely strange feeling, and the first time it happened it took me entirely by surprise. I wondered why, yet again, no one had bothered to mention that if I got a cough this would happen.

Saturday 10th December 2011

I woke up to a very cold house. The central heating had broken and the radiators weren't working. Great! I had been told to keep the boob warm (it was like having a new baby. Keep it warm, keep it fed …) and now I had no heating in the middle of winter. So, I used a hot water bottle to keep it warm in the absence of the central heating. You don't realise just how much you appreciate your heating until you don't have it. I had to keep my boob warm to prevent any pain, as it did not like the cold. Thank God I had a fire downstairs, but I struggled to sit downstairs all day, as the pain was eased only by lying in bed.

I had managed to keep my pain under control with diclofenac and paracetamol, which was not bad considering how long I was post major surgery. But then I developed an upset stomach. I think it must have been all the medication I was taking. Whatever next? In my opinion, there is nothing worse than having an upset stomach in front of your partner. Now ladies, I do not know about you, but I think it's rude to pass wind, trump or leave a nasty smell in the toilet when you are in the company of others, especially your other half! But my upset stomach became worse and the more I tried to hold the wind in, the larger my stomach got as the gas built up. I had to keep the bathroom window wide open when it was so cold outside and it was all extremely hard work. I did however work out that if I wafted the bathroom door with the window wide open, it helped to move any lingering smells faster. But my God, did I wish I could lie in peace and fart away! If I could get rid of the build-up of wind, it would ease the pain. I yearned to just let my body do whatever it needed to do without being judged!

Who started the rumour that girls don't poo or fart? Guess what boys: we do! But I still couldn't do it in front of Jed. I just wished he would fuck off for the day so I could relax, pass wind, and feel better! In the end I told him that to keep infection down he had to use a different toilet to me, and he believed me, I think! So at least I was able to have my own toilet to do my own thing (which we won't go into.) In fact, they do say that following chemotherapy you should try not to share a toilet and if you have to, you should flush it twice and only ever with the toilet lid down. So, I wasn't really lying … I was going to have chemotherapy, so I decided I might as well get him in the habit now. It's that old girl guide motto: be prepared!

As the day went on, I noticed my skin under the dressings was getting sore around the drain and wound site. When Jed looked, he noticed large blisters underneath the dressings. We sent a photo to Nurse Sandy (yes, you get their phone numbers in case you need them), who advised us to remove the dressings. At 9pm I asked my mum to come and remove them for me. Jed had been to the late-night chemist to get some fresh dressings for me. When my mum removed the dressings, it revealed that my skin had large, painful blisters and was very red and sore. I had suffered an allergic reaction to the dressings and two of the blisters had burst. It was very painful and it was just such a relief to get the dressings off. I never knew I was allergic to Tegaderm and plasters. You learn something new every day!

Sunday 11th December 2011

Scars

Following a disturbed sleep, I was very tired. I was expecting the district nurse to call and I decided to phone her to check she was actually coming. I really needed my dressings changed again, and I still had a very upset stomach. I also had a lot of fluid building up in my back and it felt like a hot water bottle slushing about inside me. The consultant had told me that I would need this draining and to expect it, but it's still a shock when one side of your back balloons – the feeling was so strange. When I moved, I felt a swishing sensation in my back. I couldn't help but move to see what would happen. It's like when you see a sign that says, Wet Paint – Do Not Touch; of course you're going to touch it! I texted my consultant to discuss it but he assured me it was normal and said it was too soon to drain it in case of infection. He told me not to worry about it. He said that a lot. He would tell you what was going to happen. For example: you will get fluid in your back and we'll have to drain it out. Then it will probably fill back up again. But when it actually happened, he would say, 'Let's see what happens – don't worry about it.' He was laid back, but so positive and caring. For the time being I resembled the Hunchback of Notre Dame.

The nurse arrived just before lunch. She said she had been surprised when she saw my DOB; she thought that as I was a breast cancer patient, I must be an older lady (never judge a book by its cover!) When she saw my breast, she was pleasantly surprised and said that the consultant had done a fantastic job. This was the same reaction I'd had from everyone I'd shown my boob to (and believe me, there have been a lot!) She had been expecting to see a flat chest with a scar running across it.

She couldn't figure out how big my wound was (it was under a plaster that had to be kept on for another week) and said she didn't know what she was dealing with wound-wise, as she had never seen this procedure before. That was reassuring! She had icy cold hands and I nearly jumped out of my skin when she put them on me. Why don't these nurses think about warming their hands up before placing them on their patients? How many times had this happened to me? She laughed and told me it was cold outside. No shit! Feel free to warm your hands up under warm water before placing them on my body!

I was a week on from my operation and found that I had a strange urge to keep checking my journal to see what I had been doing at the same time the week before. I was reliving every minute and hour when I had been in the hospital and in theatre, thinking about what they had been doing to my body the previous week. I would check the time and then think, 'I would have been in theatre now', or 'I was in recovery at this time.' I was reliving every moment and it felt like I was experiencing all the emotions all over again. It was like Groundhog Day. It was so stressful and left me feeling very anxious.

The symptoms I was experiencing were ones associated with post-traumatic stress. It is well known that your emotions can be stronger following any type of surgery, and this can be mentally and physically challenging. A week on from my surgery I had become very emotional and all those feelings are clearly stored within me to this day. Some people get these feelings a week, a month or even years following a trauma and yes, 'trauma' is how I would describe what my body had been through. It has taken many years for me to be in the position to accept what I have been through, and it is only now that I am able to discuss it without becoming upset. Most people will suffer from some form of depression following surgery, which is entirely normal, and may experience sadness, fatigue, and irritability. These feelings usually disappear over a couple of weeks but post-op depression, if left untreated, can last for many months, as can post-traumatic stress. I am sure I had suffered from both. The post-op depression appeared whilst I was in the hospital following the surgery, and the post-traumatic stress came a week later. I don't think you can ever get over a traumatic event, but you can learn to come to terms with it. It has taken me a long time, but I am glad to say that over eight years down the line I am not suffering anymore.

The first-year anniversary was a big one for me, something I am sure is the case for many people who experience trauma or loss. I had lost a part of me, even though I'd had a reconstruction, the new boob was not exactly the same as my old boob. The brain is a very powerful tool and my brain holds an image of my old boob like it does for each part of my body. This new boob with its strange sensations, the new scars, the different shape, needs to be accepted by both my brain and myself. My old boob could be touched without me feeling weird sensations in my back; my old boob fitted fully into a lacy bra that was pretty and matched my knickers! Now I have to wear underwear that doesn't always match – I cannot wear a bra anymore. I can only wear an all-in-one soft garment, as I get too much pain in the scar and drain sites to this day. My knicker drawer, which used to be a glorious mix of matching bras and knickers in all the colours of the rainbow and all styles of garments, now resembles the knicker drawer of Morticia from the Adams Family! Every garment is the exact same black all-in-one body. I can no longer wear a backless dress or bikini without my scar (which runs across my back) being on show. These scars are constant reminders of what trauma my body has endured. Don't get me wrong: I am happy with my scars as they are part of me and show the battle I have been through and survived. I am proud to be a breast cancer survivor, but before cancer I had a lovely back and now, with its scars, it just looks different.

Scars on show are always a talking point, whether that's to your face or behind your back and it reminds me of an incident when I was very heavily pregnant with my son.

It's nothing to do with scars but you'll get the gist! My hands and fingers had swollen so much that I could no longer wear my wedding ring, so I chose to wear it around my neck on my necklace. One night, the day before I gave birth, I was sitting in a restaurant celebrating my 21st birthday. The restaurant was very cosy with the tables placed very closely together. A lady from the table next to me was "discreetly" telling her husband (quite loudly), there is a very heavily pregnant lady sitting behind you, (me) but she is not wearing her wedding ring as her fingers are too swollen. Her rings are around her neck (makes the actions of pointing to her finger and then her neck), so she is obviously married but just too fat (makes actions of large belly) to get her rings on.

She was very dramatic with all the hand actions and her mouth was saying every word so slowly and in an over-exaggerated way as she tried to say each word quietly. Everyone in the tiny restaurant was now looking at me as you could hear every word this lady was saying. I could see them looking and giggling and talking to the each other – more about this lady than at me, as she was so bad at trying to be discreet. Some people just like to point out other people's flaws and that day, my flaw was being swollen from top to toe!

The incident made me sure that people must be curious when they see my back scar and wonder what type of surgery had caused me to have it (it's impressive even if I do say so myself!).

As frustrated as I was about my new boob and scars, I was also very frustrated as I couldn't do much due to my arm not having full mobility back. So, I started to use my toes to pick things up. This was tricky at first but eventually, after a bit of practice, you adapt and overcome; your toes become your fingers. For anything on the floor that needed picking up I would have to use my toes, and only every now and again did I forget about my arm and hand not working properly. However, I was soon to be reminded when a task went wrong: on one occasion I wanted to move a vase of flowers. As I lifted the vase up, I realised just how weak my arm was. I couldn't take the weight of the vase and it slipped straight out of my hand and on to the floor. What a mess! There was water and flowers everywhere – it was so frustrating.

Another time I tried to make myself a cup of tea, but the kettle was too heavy and as I tried to pour the water into my cup using my left hand (my weaker hand), the kettle fell and boiling water spilt all over the floor. I was lucky I didn't burn myself. We forget how lucky we are having the use of our arms and hands and it was times like these that made me appreciate all those little things. We take it for granted that because we are able bodied, it will always be that way. And when something happens and you lose the ability to use that limb, it really makes you stop and think.

Over a week later I noticed that my left armpit was becoming very hairy and needed a bit of love and attention. I was not allowed to shave the right armpit at that point so that just had to be left natural. And because my right arm was still not working as it should, I was unable to lift it to hold the shaver and shave the left one. Instead, I had to ask Jed to shave it for me. Now, considering men shave more or less every-day, wouldn't you think they'd be experts at it? Think again! He was like a nervous teenage boy shaving bum fluff off his chin for the first time. He was so nervous (which made me nervous) but eventually, between us, we got through the mass of hair and I at least had one nice clean-shaven armpit at the end of it! When he asked, 'Do you want me to do your legs?' he got a firm 'NOOOO!' before he'd even wrapped his tongue around the last word! Anyway … what was wrong with my legs? They weren't that hairy, were they? Oh OK, maybe a little, but I could manage those myself!

Monday 12th December 2011

A good day. I felt so much better and even managed to get in and out of the bath unaided. I could still feel the fluid swishing around in my back and when I coughed, my back still went into a spasm, and the fluid would jump with the pressure from the sneeze. There were so many new experiences to learn to live with. My brain was still struggling to adjust and accept these new strange feelings. My back muscle, which was now a boob but still attached to my back, wanted to go back to where it belonged (in my back), if that makes sense? It kept pulling itself under my armpit. This was a bizarre sensation and looked very strange as the boob contracted and twisted to the side. I had also managed to do my arm exercises quite easily and could now do twenty 'rock the baby', whoop whoop! And I was pleased with myself as I had managed to dress myself and put a jumper on without help. Look at me go: an independent adult!

What I was still having trouble with though, was spraying perfume on because I still had no strength in my right arm. Each time I tried to spray the perfume, the bottle fell over. I tried placing it on a flat surface and using my left hand to push the dispenser down, but the bottle just slipped and fell over. I tried placing it between my legs to hold it and spraying it with my left hand but by the time I bend down into the spray, the perfume had all gone. I tried holding it under my right armpit and using my left hand to push the dispenser, but the spray ended up in my mouth! So, I gave up until I could get some help. When Jed came in, he said I smelt nice and I suppose I did; after all, I had perfume in my mouth, on my fingers and in the air around me!

One of my friends, Pre, came to visit me, which was nice. She had bought me a huge bar of chocolate that we couldn't wait to devour. I hadn't eaten chocolate in such a long time.

We went into the kitchen to make a nice cup of tea to go with it. Chocolate and tea is a perfect combination, especially when you dip the chocolate into your tea and suck it! But when we came back into the lounge we were devastated: there were the remains of the chocolate bar on the floor with the wrapper ripped open and my dog was desperately guzzling as much of it as possible before we took it off her. How she had even managed to reach it from the arm of the sofa when she couldn't normally get up there (she's only small) was beyond me. I just hoped it wouldn't make her sick. I know if I had eaten a bar of chocolate that size, I would have been! And I was so desperate and looking forward to that bar of chocolate, I would have quite happily felt sick for a few hours after – it so would have been worth it. How disappointing!

Pre had been very worried about me and this was her first visit to see me since my surgery. She had been reluctant to look at my new boob, as she was scared of what she would see. I admit there was a lot of bruising, so my boob was all sorts of colours, from yellow to purple, and it was still swollen, but otherwise it looked really good. I had been using arnica tablets to help with the bruising and they appeared to be working.

When she looked, she was shocked at how good it looked and said she was very impressed. She said she'd had images of big scars across my flat chest or an ugly-looking boob. I think this was the image most people had when they heard the word 'mastectomy' so she was very pleasantly surprised.

The development of mastectomy surgery has seen massive breakthroughs. Innovations in technique have changed both the way breast cancer is managed and what surgery is now readily available. The changes from the first mastectomy – performed in the 19th century – to the surgery now being performed, and the surgery performed on me, is dramatic. Treatment is continually evolving with superior cosmetic results and this shows the strides that have been made in both medicine and surgical treatment. I was very lucky to have had a nipple-sparing mastectomy, which keeps the nipple and areola intact. This provides a great cosmetic result so a big thank you to my consultant.

Pre

I remember the night you told me you had cancer - it was the day before my birthday. You sent me the news in a text message as you had been unable to contact me. I was in shock when I read it. I didn't think it could happen to someone I knew and loved. I'm proud to say you've always remained positive and are one of the strongest people I know. I was frightened to see you after your operation, as I didn't know what I was going to see, and I was so upset for you. I was shocked at the reconstruction you had had, you looked amazing!

Tuesday 13th December 2011

A Trip to Ann Summers

My fluid-filled back was now so swollen that my extra-large bra no longer fitted. I was very uncomfortable with lots of pain and discomfort and by that evening I was back on tramadol. I had to wear a bra 24/7 for support, but unless I could find an extra-extra-large bra suitable for either Shrek's wife – Princess Fiona, or Quasimodo, I wasn't sure how it was going to be possible!

It was to be a shopping trip with a difference – I needed to get a bra that fitted me around my back. Due to the amount of swelling I now had in my back, I was a lot, lot bigger than I had been. I had skipped my bath in the morning as I couldn't have a bath and go shopping in one day; it would have left me shattered. However, when we made it to the shops, I wouldn't let the bra fitting specialist see me. The reasons were twofold:

1. I had not had a bath or shower
2. My right armpit was still very hairy and didn't smell too pleasant!

I struggled getting around town as there were lots of people Christmas shopping and I was walking like an old lady – slightly bent over and slowly shuffling along – which was tiring. I had to keep stopping for little rests and try and avoid being bumped into, which wasn't easy with so many people about. It seemed that everyone was on a mission with armfuls of bags full of Christmas present and goodies. They all knew where they wanted to go and it was full steam ahead and God help anyone who got in their way!

As always, Marks and Spencer was really busy, and we had to fight our way through the throng of people to reach the lingerie department. The bra-fitting lady measured me and was very helpful. Everything we tried on though was the wrong size. The cup size fitted but the width of my back was causing problems. It took ages trying different bras on but in the end nothing fitted. I needed bra extenders due to the swelling on my back, however, believe it or not, Marks and Spencer didn't have any bra extenders. The nice lady working in the lingerie section said she would pick me some up from the Trafford Centre but I couldn't wait a few more days and I couldn't guarantee when one of us could get back in to collect them, so I declined her kind offer. In the end, I chose a bra that fitted at the front but not the back, so until I got bra extenders, I wouldn't be able to wear it anyway.

The queues for the tills were so long with Christmas shoppers but the lady from the lingerie department put us straight to the front of one of the queues, which was great. I didn't have the energy to queue – I was now quite exhausted. The queue-jumping caused people to stare and mutter things but who cares? I was now so bloody tired again I just wanted to get home. And anyway, it's nearly Christmas people, so stop your jibber jabbering! Where's your Christmas spirit?

As we were heading back to the car, we noticed the Ann Summers shop and decided to have a quick look, just in case they sold bra extenders, nothing else! So, Jed and Mum followed me in. I have to say, being in this shop with Jed was uncomfortable enough, but to have my mum with us was bizarre! The lingerie was at the front of the shop (thank God) as this meant we didn't have to go to the back of the shop, where the battery operated and 'novelty' items were found. I wouldn't have known where to look if I had been in that section with my mum!

We couldn't find what we were looking for and when the young girl behind the counter asked if there was anything in particular we were after, I wondered for a split second what she must have thought of the three people in front of her. I don't imagine we looked like the typical Ann Summer Christmas shopper. Jed averted his eyes, whereas Mum's eyes were wide in shock, wondering where the hell we'd brought her, and I was just so tired I was shuffling along like a little old lady past the crotchless panties and peekaboo bras. I just wanted to get out of there!

Then my dad rang Mum to see where we were, which made a surreal situation even more surreal. There I was, listening to my mum tell him loudly, 'We're just in Ann Summers getting a bra-extender for Carolann. It's a shop that sells … well, everything for couples, I think.'

Everyone in the shop stared at me, including two girls who were laughing and holding up two vibrators as they tried to work out which was the best value for money! Jed didn't know where to look and continued to keep his eyes down.

I said to the assistant, 'We were looking for bra extenders but you don't appear to have any.' To which she replied, 'Yes we do – they're just over here, follow me.'

She led me to the back of the shop, past all the vibrators and sex toys with Jed and my mum in tow. Why would they put the bra extenders with the vibrators? It makes no sense. Surely bra extenders should be with the bras?

Anyway, the staff in Ann Summers were brilliant and fitted two bra extensions for me. Can you believe it? I was so swollen, that one bra extender wasn't enough; they had to fasten two together and gave me a third in case I needed it. How embarrassing – it was a Bridget Jones moment! Never would I have imagined I would find myself in Ann Summers with Jed, my mum, and my dad on the phone! It turned into a proper family shopping expedition but it was a job well done.

On the way out, Mum turned to me and said quietly, 'Did you see those bras and knickers with all the holes in? Fancy selling ripped underwear! Is that the new look, like wearing jeans with holes in the knees? Do you think Jenna would like some for Christmas?

I answered, 'No Mum. And definitely, no Mum!'

By the time I got home I was absolutely shattered. The whole trip had taken its toll and by the time we got home I had to go straight to bed to have a little sleep. The fluid in my back was getting worse and I now looked even more like Quasimodo than Quasimodo himself! This was getting ridiculous – it felt like I was lying on a water bed and I could hear the slushing sound as it moved about! When I told my consultant, he still said, 'Don't worry, let's see what happens if we just leave it; we'll see if your body reabsorbs it.'

I thought, if we leave it much longer, I'll need sending

to the juicer! He did turn out to be right though. I'm sure he used me as a guinea pig, trying different new methods out, but it always turned out OK. Everything he tried, including leaving the nipple on, keeping the back muscle attached to the back, and leaving the fluid to reabsorb all worked out for my benefit in the end. He was such a clever man.

For the time being though, my back was very swollen and I had to just hope and pray my body would start to reabsorb it sooner rather than later!

Wednesday 14th December 2011
It Always Happens to Me

The nurse came to change my bandages today. She was very nice but unfortunately for me she had bad breath. Each time she had spoken to me I'd struggled not to gag as her rancid breath made contact with my nostrils. And yes, it was *rancid*, not like a normal bad breath, which is bad enough. I'm one of those people who have a sensitive gag reflex and unfortunately cannot suppress it. When my body doesn't like a smell or taste, it makes sure that everyone around knows this, by making this involuntary gagging action. It's actually quite embarrassing.

The nurse was very close to me, changing the dressings on both my boob and my back, so there was no way of avoiding the smell and I didn't want to be rude and tell her she had really bad breath. It took all my willpower and a bit of holding my breath, which I am not very good at, before I could hold it in no longer: I gagged out loud, making a sound that resembled someone about to be sick. She asked if I was OK. I couldn't say *no, your breath stinks* so I just told her I was feeling very nauseous. In hindsight, I think I preferred the cold hands!

Speaking of the cold, the heating was still not working properly and the only place to keep warm was my bed. So off I shuffled to the bedroom, looking forward to lying in my bed and watching television.

When I got to the bedroom door, I was surprised to see it was closed. I wouldn't normally close it as the lock wasn't working and therefore when you closed the door completely, it locked from the inside. I tried the handle but it wouldn't budge. The door was locked from the inside. My granddaughter had been playing with it the night before and had tried to lock it, which was OK when we were inside the bedroom as you could open it from there, but she must have moved the bolt over a touch and when my mum had closed the door that morning it had somehow locked from the inside. Nothing would open that door! I was now locked out of my bedroom for the day until Jed came home from work and fixed it.

I had to rest on the sofa and because the house was so cold with no heating, I had blankets and a hot water bottle. At least there was a fire in the living room to help keep us warm. And we had the telly on so we could watch our afternoon programmes, so it was not too bad. It felt a bit like glamping, something I had always wanted to try but had never been brave enough. This little taster would give me an insight into the world of glamping.

Unfortunately, as Mum was dusting, she accidently pulled the wires out of the back of the telly. Between us we couldn't work out how to fix it and I couldn't bend to look behind the telly to see which wire went where, so we were stuck with no TV for the rest of the day. It really was like glamping now; no TV, no bed, no clothes, or make-up. I was really roughing it!

Pain had started to creep into my back as I'd been sitting up too long and I needed some pain relief. But all my medication was locked up safely in my bedroom. So, with no pain relief and only the heat from the fire and no TV to watch, we had to rough it for the rest of the afternoon. This insight into glamping confirmed what I always suspected: I needed my luxuries so it was a definite no-no!

I had however invited a beautician to come to the house that day, which was a bonus. I was still in my pyjamas as my clothes were locked in my bedroom, along with my make-up, which made opening the door to a stranger in the middle of the afternoon with no make-up on a bit embarrassing. If you knew me, you'd know I never go out in public without make-up, especially lipstick.

She looked me up and down, eyeing my pyjamas, then made eye contact and said, 'Hello I'm your beautician.'

She didn't comment on the pyjamas, but then, what could she say?' Wow, your pyjamas look amazing!'

I apologised for the cold house, my lack of clothes and the fact that my hair and make-up were non-existent. And obviously, she was pristinely turned out – all beauticians always are!

Over the course of the afternoon, I had a French polish on my toes, and mum had her eyebrows and eyelashes tinted. It was really nice having these treatments at home as it gave us something to do, especially now we had no TV to watch! And on the plus side, although my hair and face were a mess, my feet looked good. Maybe this glamping lark was not as bad as I first thought. Maybe I should recall the words to *I Love to Go a-Wandering* and *Ging Gang Goolie* just in case!

By late afternoon, and because I'd been up all day, the pain in my back had become really bad. I was very swollen and getting larger by the hour. I really needed to lie flat in my bed. All my pain relief was locked away in my bedroom so, apart from some paracetamol, which was not strong enough to get on top of the pain, there was nothing else I could take. We were looking forward to Jed getting home from work more than ever so he could fix the telly and get me back into my bedroom. Come on Jed– hurry home!

Thursday 15th December 2011

I had a great night's sleep the previous night. It was 9am before I woke. I am *loving* these good nights' sleep. And no more strange dreams. I was on my own in the morning so had to make my own breakfast (yes, I said that). Jed had kindly filled the kettle, knowing I couldn't lift it to fill it and he had put just enough water in it for a couple of brews (so thoughtful). The house was still really cold. Why could the electrician and plumber not find the fault? They were due back again today and I was really hoping they would find the problem this time. They had been to the house three times already and had been unable to sort it out. It was nearly Christmas and it would be lovely to have a nice warm house – my boob for one would really appreciate it! They were like Laurel and Hardy when they came: they looked at the boiler and prodded a few things and then they left. They spilt coffee on my carpet and dragged mud up the stairs but still not found the fault. Perhaps they were waiting for an invite to Christmas dinner, which I would gladly have given them if they could just fix the heating. I would get out of my warm bed or leave the warmth of the living room and as soon as I stepped a foot into the hall or kitchen, my boob would contract with the cold and hide under my arm pit and the pain in my back would be piercing. My poor body needed warmth, particularly my new boob!

I had been told not to do any washing as wet washing was too heavy for me to lift. So ... I did a wash. And yes, they were right, wet washing is extremely heavy. I couldn't pick it up off the floor. It took all my time and energy just to pull it out of the machine. Because I was on my own, I had no one telling me off when I did things I wasn't supposed to do. It was very frustrating having to wait for other people to do my washing or cleaning so I just got on with as much as I could manage.

The electrician and plumber told me they had fixed the heating at last – hurray! It had only taken them five days and four visits ... at last I could hang my washing on the radiators to get it dry, instead of struggling to hang it outside where the cold meant it wouldn't have dried anyway. It took me nearly an hour to put all the washing on different radiators and by the time I had finished I was shattered and my side was sore, so I did the sensible thing and went back to bed. Then I realised that my blister had burst and *yakkamush* (our word for an unknown horrible substance) had stuck to my pyjamas. Mum had to pull my pyjamas off the blister and ouch it hurt! *Yakkamush* is disgusting!

My consultant had warned me about my tiredness, explaining that before the surgery, my body was like a car full of petrol; I would start each day with a full tank and could manage to do everything I needed to do. By the end of the day I still had petrol left over. Post-surgery I would start the day with only half a tank of petrol and by the end of the day I would be empty. Therefore, I could not expect to do as much as I used to do on a daily basis. He was so right! I used to lead such a busy and active life. I worked full time as a nurse, ran a dance school, volunteered at a local school teaching after-school dance, and brought up my two children with energy left to go out and enjoy life. I had turned into a different person literally overnight. One day I had a great pair of matching boobs, I had no scars and my back was blemish free and I had a hectic, enjoyable, perfect life full of activity. After the surgery, I still had a great pair of boobs, thanks to my wonderful consultant, albeit that one had a mind of its own. (Though I'd soon have it trained: my back *will* become a boob!) I have scars, swelling on my back (which was getting ridiculous), and pain and discomfort on a daily basis. And most frustratingly I could only manage to do five-minute tasks before the exhaustion kicked in and I had to stop and rest or have a little sleep. I was like a baby with all the daytime naps. Prior to the surgery, I had never slept in the day time.

More than eight years on, my tank is only ever half full, and I still struggle to do everything I want to achieve in a day. I usually get to 6pm and then it's like a switch is flicked and I'm exhausted. This can happen as suddenly as a traffic light turning from amber to red. When it turns red, I have to stop, and it doesn't turn green again until the following day, so any plans to finish a task or do something in the evening is a no go. I've had to learn to adjust to this new me, and it has taken some time and work to get my brain and body to understand I'm not the super-energetic person I was before surgery, even though I desperately want to be. Instead, I'm like an old car with a new engine. My mind is still so active, but my body can't keep up. I used to love the days when my brain chemicals and hormone levels were just right, and I could enjoy every minute without having to stop to take a nap!

Friday 16th December 2011

I slept from 11pm and woke up at 9.30am following another great night's sleep. Mum had made me porridge. She makes the real porridge with sugar and milk. Mum is from Scotland, so they know how to make real porridge from oats. Jenna came over to see me and washed my hair, so I felt much better. You always feel better when your hair is clean. Today was the best day I had had so far. I had no pain so didn't need to use pain relief which was a bonus. I was being fussed over for some reason, but I wasn't going to complain as I was enjoying being well and could appreciate what Mum and Jenna were doing for me.

Then it started to snow, which was so lovely to see nine days before Christmas. Let's hope it stays until Christmas Day. A white Christmas would be perfect. I stood watching the flurries of flakes falling softly onto the back garden creating a white blanket of snow; it looked so magical. Flurries of snow twirled and danced before landing, helping create an even thicker blanket on the garden. It was mesmerising to watch. Mum joined me and said, 'I hate to tell you this, but little Tia has died.'

Tia was my little dog, a toy Yorkshire terrier, and when she was a puppy, she was so small I could fit her in my pocket. I used to sneak her into many of my lectures when I was a student nurse as I couldn't leave her all day on her own. I'd sit at the back of the lecture theatre, and no one knew she was there. She was so little and she just snuggled in my bag.

This was very sad news. She had died whilst I had been recovering from surgery and no one had told me as they had wanted me to concentrate on my recovery. Tia had been staying with my brother so he could take her out and care for her whilst I was recovering. He was so good with her and he had been with her at the end, so that was some comfort to me – I knew he loved her as much as I did, and he would have cared for her right till the end. So, this was why my mum and Jenna had been fussing over me; they had been worried about telling me.

The snow continued to fall and the day looked so perfect. Everything was clean and white with no imperfections but my heart ached with the loss of my little Tia. It was a very sad day knowing that she was gone and another chapter of life was over. She had been part of the family for twelve years. Sleep well little Tia.

To top the day off I received another bill from the private hospital. This time £3.50 for a sandwich I never had! I had no intention of paying it.

Saturday 17th December 2011

It was our annual dance school Christmas party, but I was just too exhausted to attend, which was so frustrating as it was always a good night out. Out of curiosity I tried my new dress on and was surprised to find I could still get into it and get it fastened up (apart from the one strap across the wound on my back). My back was still very swollen, so even if I had wanted to go to the party my dress didn't fit, and it would have been a nightmare trying to find something else to wear.

I had my heart set on wearing this dress and you know what it's like when you're all ready to go out and suddenly you have a wardrobe malfunction? Well I was not ready for that sort of stress yet! I loved shopping and I loved buying new clothes, especially when I was going somewhere nice. The first time I'd seen this dress, I knew it was the one: it had shown off my lovely boobs and my little waist and it was backless with a couple of straps so it also showed off my nice back. Looking in the mirror I could now see the large bandage on my back, which didn't look great and I had sores from the blisters that had popped and left red, angry wounds. The large bulge in my back from the fluid now protruded from my side. The swelling was so big it looked like I had one of those skin expanders that they place under the skin when they need the skin to stretch and grow. Regardless, I could not have gone out anyway; by 8pm I would have been exhausted and by 9pm I would have been asleep!

I really wanted to enjoy the run up to Christmas and if I couldn't go out and celebrate, then I would celebrate at home with Jed. We sat downstairs in the lounge and switched off all the lights, leaving just the Christmas-scented candles on and the Christmas tree lights. It was all very cosy, and we had a relaxing night in watching good old cheesy Christmas television programmes with a glass of mulled wine, and a Bailey's. It was a perfect night in, and I lasted till 9pm when I became so tired, I had to go bed! Anyway, who over the age of 40 really wants to go out at Christmas when it is cold and busy? You have to fight to get to the bar to order your drink and that's after you've managed to get past the doormen who seem to think they're all FBI agents. They scrutinise what you're wearing (what's wrong with a polo neck? It's winter for God's sake!) The last time I went to a club I thought I had walked into a nursery. How young were all the kids there? Wow, I felt so old and the only exciting thing about being in this club was the fact that it had big comfy sofas. I was just too old to be going out to certain clubs – a sad thing to say perhaps but in reality, it was true. Besides, I'm far too busy to have a hangover. They used to disappear after a few hours but these days I found they lasted up to two weeks! So, no I was quite happy sitting in my living room with my Christmas-scented candles and going to bed at nine!

Sunday 25th December 2011

At last it was Christmas Day! I loved Christmas so much. I had rested for the previous couple of days to ensure I had more energy for the big day. I had already done my Christmas shopping, (most of it last year in the January sales in fact, when you always get some great bargains) and the rest of it just before my surgery. All the presents had been wrapped since the end of November and the Christmas tree had been up since the middle of November, so I was well and truly prepared for Christmas Day! The presents spilled out from under the tree, taking over the living room. Each family member had their own wrapping paper so they would know which presents were theirs. Every year I told my children and my grandchildren, 'don't expect too much this year', but they knew that each year they would be spoiled and would say, 'I thought you said you were not going overboard this year?' But I was just as excited about giving them presents as they were receiving them.

On Christmas Eve I still struggled to go to sleep. I was so excited to see their faces in the morning when they unwrapped their presents. All those months of preparing, Christmas gift lists, shopping, finding bargains, wrapping presents, and making sure everyone had the same amount to open, and within half an hour the present unwrapping formality would be all over. Christmas wrapping paper would be strewn all over the living room, selection boxes opened, and toys and gifts placed in their little piles of ownership. Watching the scene before me – my family laughing, having fun and being together on such an occasion was a tonic for me. It was like a scene from a TV advert. They say laughter is good for the soul and they are right. Life doesn't get any better than this. I had all my family around me, and they were all healthy, safe, and happy, and I was on the way to recovery. No amount of money could buy this happiness and there is no amount of money in this world that can buy perfect health. I am the richest person I know as I have everything: family, friends, happiness, and perfect health. I am so lucky!

We had originally booked to have Christmas dinner at a nearby restaurant, something we do most years. Jenna, Ryan and the grandchildren still went as it was all paid for. I had managed to get a refund for Jed and myself so we stayed at home and my mum made us a lovely Christmas dinner. I just lay on the settee being waited on hand and foot; it was like being a child all over again.

We had a quiet afternoon, just my mum, dad, Jed and me. It was a lovely day though and one I will always remember. Having all my family around in the morning for the present-opening ceremony, and then having my mum's home-cooked Christmas dinner (which was just delicious) had brought back all my lovely childhood Christmas memories. It was a very special treat as we do not get to spend Christmas with my mum normally, so it was an extra special Christmas for me and one that I will always cherish. I did experience a bit of pain and discomfort throughout the day, and I was left feeling very tired, but it had been a perfect family Christmas and I couldn't have asked for anything to make it any more special. We were all so blessed to have each other and for the wonderful Christmas Day we were given.

I had another memorable Christmas that I must share with you: one year our whole family went to Tenerife for Christmas. Jenna and Ryan were teenagers so beyond the stage of believing in Father Christmas. (Well, Jenna was – ha! We had managed to keep the magic for my son till he was well into secondary school). This was the first time we had been away from home at Christmas and it was lovely to be able to sit around the pool and listen to Christmas songs. The sun was shining, and everything was perfect. There had been no stress and Christmas dinner was cooked for us in the restaurant, so all we had to do was relax until it was ready. Perfect.

We had decorated the apartment with some tinsel from home and found a large palm leaf, which we decorated with cuttings from the wrapping paper. There were Santa faces, snowmen, and stars. We placed the decorated palm in our apartment and put some little fairy lights around it. When we switched the lights on, we noticed a little lizard on the palm. It sat very still at the top of the palm leaf, where the angel or star would have been and didn't seem fazed or scared by what we were doing.

Following a perfect Christmas day, we went to bed as normal. I was sleeping in the living room area of the apartment and my family were using the bedrooms. I had a pull-down bed settee and behind it six steps led up to a small landing which led in turn to the front door.

In the early hours of the morning I woke with the strange feeling that someone was in the room with me. I didn't know what time it was, but it must have been early as it was still quite dark in the apartment. A small amount of light filtered through the glass of the front door, cast from the lamp post outside. I looked behind me at the steps and saw, I believed, my dad. I thought nothing of it at first as he always went for an early morning run. Usually he just got up and went out without waking anyone else so why was he just standing on the second step and staring at me? This was weird. I asked him what was wrong but he didn't respond. He just continued to stare. I sat up in my bed and let my eyes adjust to the light. I looked closer at him but something wasn't right. My heart began to beat faster, which is never a good sign. What on earth was he wearing? He looked like a soldier. Then realisation hit me: this was not my dad; he was far too tall for a start and he certainly didn't wear clothes like that! I screamed like I always did when confronted with a paranormal image, and grabbed for the lamp, which luckily was right next to me.

By the time I had switched it on and looked up again,

he had vanished. It had all happened so quickly. I was so scared, even more so than on previous occasions. I put the main light on in the lounge and did my usual stupid check of the apartment, alone in semi darkness, to make sure the front door was locked, and no one had broken in.

It was 4am, far too early for my dad to go out running. I checked on Jenna and Ryan who were fast asleep and noticed the door to my mum's bedroom was closed and my dad's running shoes were still next to the front door, confirming he was still in bed. My heart was still beating fast and I could feel it hammering against my chest. Everything was locked and we were all safe from intruders but not, it seemed, from paranormal entities!

I had to sleep with the light on for the rest of the night, not that I got much sleep; I did manage another couple of hours of broken sleep before I heard the door close as my dad went out for his early morning run at 6.30am.

I told my family about my Christmas night ghostly visit and none of them could provide an explanation for what I had seen. Luckily, we were leaving to go home that day, which I have to say I was very relieved about because I didn't want to spend another night in that apartment. This sighting had really shaken me up and I was still feeling very scared even though the figure was gone, it was now daylight and I had people around me. I wonder why they only ever come when I am alone. I don't know if I was feeling scared because I was in unfamiliar surroundings when I saw him or if it was the aura I had felt, or because he had been so real and close to me – too close. Whatever the reason, I just wanted to get out. I packed our things up as quickly as I could, and I think my urgency scared Jenna and Ryan as they'd never seen me that frightened before. We later found out from the owner that the apartments were built on land where many a battle had been fought during the Anglo-Spanish war. What was it with soldiers coming back to see me? My very own Christmas ghost and one of the scariest to date!

Tuesday 27th December 2011

Poo

So, enough of this relaxing and taking it easy; it was time to walk off some of the Christmas calories (though I wouldn't have the energy to walk them all off!). I was feeling good following a couple of days rest, so we decided to go into town to have a walk around. It was very busy as, once again, the sales were on and people were out shopping. It was not an easy task making sure I wasn't bumped into. I was so worried so that someone would bump into my back or my breast, which was still very tender. Normally I would be in the thick of it buying my Christmas wrapping paper, advent calendars and half-price perfumes for the next year, but not this year. It was just too busy and the queues were far too long. Occasionally, I had to sit down on a bench to have a rest. I couldn't believe how exhausting it was just having this short walk. It really took it out of me, but I did manage to stay out all day, which was an achievement. I liked being out and about as it made me feel like I was back to normal life again. As exhausted as I was my pain wasn't too bad and I didn't have to take any pain relief throughout the day. This was another achievement and proved that I was well on the road to recovery.

Now I know we ladies do not like having conversations about our bowels, but for some reason men do. So, this next entry would have some men in their element, who love nothing more than discussing their toilet habits. Some even leave traces of their bowel and toilet habits for us ladies to see what they have been up to! And then it is down to us to clean up after them. It's like having a newly toilet-trained toddler! Why do men do this? I would be mortified leaving a dirty toilet or peeing on the pan and leaving it for someone else to clean up! This is not my Jed though as I have him well and truly trained. When I first met Jed, I gave him a short list of what I expected in a man and if there was anything on the list he could not meet, then he was not the man for me! I was too old to have to start re-training another man, so I needed one who was already *partly trained*; a bit rough around the edges was okay as long as he was happy to be tweaked! And number one on my list was this: I do not want to see or smell what you have been up to on the toilet!

Other stipulations included not wanting any more children, not wanting to get married, a non-smoker, good teeth, great personality, and someone who could make me laugh. The list was more extensive than this, but you get the gist! The list worked as we each knew exactly what we were looking for in a relationship. We knew what little habits would annoy us so it was all out in the open before we got serious, and I can honestly say we have never had a cross word or an argument in all the years we have been together. So, a list (a bit like a shopping list) is the way forward if you have not yet found your Mr Right!

So, I must share with you my deep secret: today I managed to open my bowels and have a poo all on my own with no constipation and no laxative mediation to help me, which is always a bonus. I had been having 'bottom troubles' since my operation and twenty-three days later I had finally managed to go all on my own, so it was worth a mention as it was a big achievement … excuse the pun!

Fact: did you know that stools can be classified into one of seven shapes? I remember as a student nurse we were given a stool chart. For anyone interested here are the seven shapes:

1. Separate hard lumps (severe constipation).
2. Sausage shaped but lumpy (mild constipation).
3. A sausage shape with cracks on its surface (normal).
4. Like a sausage or snake, smooth and soft (average stool normal).
5. Soft blobs with clear-cut edges (lacking fibre).
6. Mushy consistency with ragged edges (mild diarrhoea).
7. Liquid consistency with no solid pieces (severe diarrhoea).

I know: weird, but I bet our men would love this chart. And no, I'm not telling you which number mine was!

Wednesday 28th December 2011
Getting back to normality

Today was another full day that I didn't have to take any pain relief. I was so happy! I was still uncomfortable but not enough to have to take anything for it. Jed and I had decided to go out for a walk. It was a beautiful winter's day, perfect for wrapping up warm and having a stroll. I loved days like these. Today was crispy cold with a biting chilly wind, but if you were wrapped up warm you could enjoy being out in the cold air. Although the sun was out it gave a false impression as it gave no warmth or comfort, and I'd only been out for ten minutes before we had to return home. It was simply too cold for my breast! Even though I was well wrapped up, nothing was going to stop that biting wind from penetrating my boob. And the pain I experienced as the bitter wind pierced straight through me, was so terrible that it made my back and boob go into a spasm. My poor boob was trying desperately to get back into its old position, in my back. It was disappointing as I really wanted to go for a walk, but I now realised, no matter how well I wrapped up, nothing would prevent the cold penetrating my clothes and getting into my boob. I'll try and describe this pain for you as best as I can:

If you have ever burnt your hand, then you run it under cold water for ten minutes, until your hand starts to freeze and cause you pain, well, it was a bit like that.

Last summer we went to Ripley's Believe it or Not! in London and they had an interactive scene of the *Titanic*. There was an area filled with water, which was supposed to represent the icy cold water the night the *Titanic* sank. We dipped our hands into the water, and it was so bitterly cold it was painful. This was the same sensation I experienced in my breast and back when I went out in the cold.

Following our short walk, it took nearly two hours before I felt warm again. I had to wrap up in a blanket and have a hot water bottle. My back was so swollen I had to put the bra extenders on again. I made a mental note that in the future when I went out in the cold, I would take a hot water bottle with me to prevent this from happening again. (I later discovered that using stick-on heat patches worked wonders. I would place one on my back and one on my breast and this really helped).

My back felt very strange and yet it was numb to the touch. This feeling is also very hard to describe but if you've ever had a filling at the dentist and had to have an injection to numb the area, this is how my boob and back felt: numb. If that numbed area had an itch, because the area was numb you wouldn't get any relief when you scratched. It was most bizarre. When I tried to scratch my numbed breast, instead of getting relief for the itch, all I could feel was a prodding in my back. If I even lightly prodded the reconstructed breast, I would feel the prod in my back and not on the breast – it was all very confusing. And worst of all: if someone brushed by me and caught my nipple, the sensation was bizarre (and not in a nice way!) it made me squirm!

My consultant had left the new breast tissue (which use to be my back muscle) attached to the back tendons and blood vessels to secure a good blood flow and keep it alive. So, my back muscle was now in my chest trying to be a boob. No wonder it felt strange! The consultant had said it would take a couple of years for the back muscle to realise that it was now breast muscle but in fact, this has never happened. This muscle knows it's in the wrong place and lets me know on a daily basis. It will cramp up and try to return to its rightful place; it's like an ongoing game of tug of war between my back and my front!

After all my treatment had finished, I had a shock when I jumped into the deep end of the swimming pool on holiday. I can swim, at least, ordinarily I can, but on this particular day when I jumped in, I tried to do the breaststroke as normal. That was when I realised I could no longer swim! What a shock!

I tried floating, rather than panicking, largely so I didn't cause alarm or make myself look stupid; I was in no mood for being rescued and causing a scene. Floating worked so I was safe for the time being whilst I worked out what had happened to my swimming abilities.

I tried again to do the breaststroke, but my arm had no strength and my 'back boob muscle' was literally disappearing under my armpit, in its defence, trying to do its job as a back muscle to help me swim. This poor muscle was not wired up for doing the breaststroke. I tried my hardest to make it work but all I ended up doing was going around in circles as the boob pulled and did it's hardest to help me. I had to hold my boob to try to keep it in place and prevent it from protruding out of the side of my swimming costume. Either muscles have memories and this muscle was traumatised, or my brain could not compute the mix up of body parts. A bit like when someone loses a limb and the brain still thinks it's there and causes phantom pain. So, breaststroke was out for now and front crawl was a definite no-no, as I couldn't lift my arm up and pull myself through the water. Floating and treading water was all I could do and eventually I floated to the shallow end and got myself out.

For the rest of the holiday I stayed in the shallow end, strengthening and teaching my arm to swim again. No one had warned me I may not be able to swim. If they had, I would never have jumped in the deep end! But thank God I found out in the pool and not in the sea, where it could have been more serious.

The next time we were on holiday I made sure I was able to swim before going into the sea. We hired a pedalo and off we went, over the waves. I decided to have dip. The sea was crystal blue, the sun was shining and there wasn't a cloud in the sky. The water was lovely and I bobbed up and down enjoying the warmth from both the sun and the water. Jed stayed on the pedalo as he couldn't swim. Then it was time to get back onto the pedalo and this was when I discovered that my arm was too weak to pull me back on. We tried everything but there was no way I could do it. I had no upper body strength and I was stuck. Thinking quickly, I put one leg on the pedalo, so I was lying on my back in the water. The waves were quite big, and my head disappeared under each one, which didn't help. Using all my strength from both legs (thank God I have strong dancer's legs!) I managed to heave myself back onto the pedalo with Jed pulling on my good arm and my legs.

When I later asked Jed to describe what I looked like he said, 'like a Walrus trying to get on a rock!' He thought he was going to have to tow me back to shore with me clinging to the back of the pedalo. Now *that* would have been embarrassing so I've never got myself into a predicament like that again.

Anyway, because he said I resembled a Walrus, I'll tell you about Jed's mishap: as I said, he can't swim and one sunny day we were on the beach and he needed to change his swimming shorts (or in his case his floating shorts). I told him to go into the water and change them, that way no one would see him. Because he's so tall, he had to go out quite far, which is dangerous when you can't swim and the sea is rough. As he pulled his shorts off and tried to put his foot into the new pair, a wave knocked him right off his feet and he ended up under the water naked and panicking. He took in water each time he screamed. I tried to help – really, I did – but he was too heavy and I was laughing so much it was hard to focus. I had to concentrate on not weeing in the sea as I was laughing so hard and that took much of my effort. Jed was thrashing his arms around, thinking he was going to drown. I shouted to him to stand up and when he did, he realised that he was standing in only three feet of water. If I could put crying emojis in here I would – it was the funniest thing I've ever seen. Remember what he was doing before he got knocked over? Yes, he now stood in three feet of water in nothing but his birthday suit! 'Walrus', did you say, Jed …?

Over the coming months there were many things I was to discover I could no longer do due to lack of strength in my arm and upper body. I felt as though I was wired up wrong. Unfortunately, the surgery didn't come with a manual of what you can and cannot do, so it was just trial and error, which was quite scary for me at times. I had to learn to expect the unexpected, which was funny (mainly for those around me), humiliating at times and, occasionally, a little dangerous. I just had to find out what I could and couldn't do, as and when I tried to do it. The only things I'd been told I wouldn't be able to do following the surgery was pole dancing and rock climbing. Consequently, we took down the poles and gave up rock climbing!

Sneezing I discovered early on, was another problem I had to overcome. Every time a sneeze came on, I had to hold my boob to prevent it going into a spasm and retreating under my armpit. It reminded me of a tortoise putting its head into its shell when it was scared. My boob was the same: anything it didn't like, it hid from in the safety of my armpit. And I never realised just how many times a day I coughed. Each time I coughed, even in public, my hand would automatically hold my boob in protection. Most people put their hands to their mouths when they cough; I put mine on my boob! This was one of the most bizarre feelings I experienced on a daily basis. And as much as I didn't like any of these sensations, I have had to accept that they are now part of my life. I'm reminded on a daily basis when I do any tasks that involve using my right arm or upper body, even many years later, that I have had an anatomy-changing procedure. So, my consultant was actually wrong when he said, it would take two years for the back muscle to realise it was now a breast muscle – it still doesn't. There was no fooling my muscle; it knew it was wired back to front and it will never forgive my consultant for making those changes, or let me forget it was not happy being a boob instead of a back. Not many people can say they have a 'back muscle boob'!

I decided I would deserve a holiday once this is all over. I fancied going to Cyprus. That is what I would focus on during my chemo. It will help me to get through it. And it would be a holiday of a lifetime. I needed to get my chemo out of the way first though, one step at a time.

And that is exactly what we did: as soon as the chemo was over, we booked our holiday of a lifetime to Cyprus. I made sure I was spoilt rotten with a five-star hotel and treatment to match. I was enjoying having my life back so much and I was eager to try out new things in life, things I would not normally have done.

After that we had two trips to Australia to see my son who was performing on the cruise ships, and he got us zip-wiring across the cruise ship; standing on top of the big screen on the ship as it sailed out of Sydney Harbour; walking the plank over the sea (we got to stand on the very edge of the ship, where we then recreated the famous scene from *Titanic*); we even went zorbing! We were driven to the top of a very steep hill, put into a large inflatable ball, got freezing cold water chucked on us before we were pushed down the hill and bounced around in the ball – all things that got your heart racing. And it made me feel alive. I was so lucky to be living again. At the age of forty-three I felt a whole new lease of life and I was going to enjoy every moment. I would never had tried zorbing prior to the cancer. I would have been too scared. But now I was taking chances and pushing my boundaries. Life started to feel like the islands we visited whilst we were in Australia: perfect, beautiful and untouched. Life doesn't get any better.

For now, though I had to concentrate on getting my body as strong and healthy as I could, in preparation for my fight with the chemo … *dun dun dunnn!* I knew I had to strengthen my nails, so I'd been using nail hardener everyday trying to get them as strong as I could before the chemo weakened and damaged them. The nurse had warned me about my nails and hair. She said I would lose my hair after about eleven days (I don't think so – this will *not* be happening to me) and that I would possibly lose my toenails (which is disgusting. There was no way I was going to allow that to happen either.). She said I would get three lines in my fingernails, one for each of the last three chemos I would have. They would be a bit like battle scars – one stripe for each session of chemo I had fought and conquered.

I was bloody determined to hold on to my hair and

nails though, and I had a few little tricks up my sleeve. Little did I know at the time, I was about to enter a battle with the biggest, strongest kick-arse poisons I would ever meet in my life, and no little tricks up my sleeve would be strong enough to prevent what was about to happen.

My body was still tired but my brain was so active. I just wanted to be back to normal and be able to do more. It was so frustrating. The more my body healed, the more I felt I should be back to normal but the tiredness, or should I say exhaustion, was just too strong for me to fight against. My scars were looking great, although they were a bit dry and I was using Savlon cream to soften them up. It was quite itchy around the scars, which was good as it shows they were healing. My right arm looked fat though, like I had suddenly developed bingo wings and, compared to my left arm, it looked as though I had fluid in it. I didn't like the look of it and just hoped I wasn't developing lymphedema, something that can be caused from having your lymph nodes removed. I had to do more arm-strengthening exercises to prevent this from happening. There was no way this was going to happen to me, so I upped the amount of exercises I was already doing and made this my next mission.

Thursday 29th December 2011

Well some people shave their hair off. Some record the event and raise money at the same time as they prepare themselves for the inevitable: becoming bald. Not me. I was not going to shave my hair off for anyone and I was determined I wouldn't lose it either. There *had* to be a way of preventing hair loss whilst having chemo. It was just that no one had discovered it yet. Maybe I could be the one to discover how – now that *would* be exciting! One thing was for sure: I was going to do everything in my power to ensure I kept my hair for as long as I could.

The first part of my plan was to go to the hairdressers and get my hair cut just that little bit shorter. Having it shorter meant I could manage it during the second part of my master plan.

We went to a hairdresser I hadn't used before and she did a great job. She was very nice and used extra towels to make padding for my back when she washed my hair as I was sore when leaning back. She did what she could to make me feel comfortable and I loved my new hairstyle, not that it would stay like that for long, which was a shame.

Friday 30th December 2011

Today's task was to get everything I would need for my chemo lockdown. I had been advised to get drinks and snacks and, obviously, new pyjamas, comfy clothes, and slippers for all the days of rest I was to have.

It was nice shopping again, even though it was only for items to wear when I was going to be unwell. I would much rather have been shopping for holiday clothes – that would have been so much more fun. Jetting off somewhere nice and warm would have been a dream but it wasn't worth thinking about that now. It would happen once I got over this next hurdle. I could not believe I was back here again, feeling quite well and yet knowing I was going to be ill again. I didn't like preparing to be unwell; I just wanted to be healthy and to stay healthy.

It was very busy in the shops with people still shopping for bargains in the sales. You couldn't put a hand out in front of you without touching someone it was so busy. Jed was very protective and had his arm out in front of me the whole time, making sure no one bumped into me.

I had a sudden urge to see my mum. I hadn't spoken to her that day so had no idea what she was up to. I told Jed I wanted to go to the Indian buffet restaurant that we had been to once before. He was shocked at my choice of restaurant as we'd not had a good experience last time, we went there but I chose it because I had a strong feeling my mum would be there. I don't know why I thought she would be at this restaurant, but as always, I followed my gut instinct.

When we arrived at the restaurant, I was disappointed to see my mum's car wasn't there. Was my gut instinct wrong this time? Strange – it had never let me down before. Maybe she would turn up; I still had a strong feeling that she would. However, when we walked in, I was surprised to see that not only was the restaurant quiet for a lunch time, but there were only two other people inside: my mum and dad! They were as shocked to see us as we were them. They had decided to pop in for lunch simply because they'd been passing. They were on their way home, having being out for a drive.

We spent a lovely couple of hours catching up, though the food was not very good. The buffet was cold the first time we came and it was just as cold the second time. That was the reason we'd said we would never come back. Mum had done the same thing. She said they'd only popped in as they were passing and thought they would give it another chance. I told you my gut instinct was always right; once again, it didn't fail. But we wouldn't be returning to eat here again, regardless of what my gut told me!

The last time I'd had such a powerful gut feeling was when I was about eight years old. I was in Scotland with my brother, who was a couple of years older than me. My cousins were all going up to visit my gran in Easter House, but they were all older than me and my auntie didn't want me to go as she thought I was too young. (She didn't know I knew this though as she didn't say anything about it to me. She was obviously worried about me, which was understandable.)

I just knew something wasn't right. I could feel in the pit of my stomach that something was going to happen. I was standing at the bus stop with my brother and cousins when I felt a strong feeling come over me: I knew the minute I stepped onto the bus, my auntie was going to pull me back and stop me going. I didn't see the image in my head, I just felt it.

I looked around to see if I could see her, and although she was nowhere in sight, I just knew what was going to happen. I kept looking around, still I couldn't see her. I was getting anxious at the thought of what was about to happen. I couldn't speak and I was starting to feel sick. Was I imagining this or was this actually going to happen? And, if so, where was she?

My cousins and brother were talking and acting normally. They weren't aware of anything out of the ordinary. The bus arrived and I prepared myself for the inevitable. My heart was racing. As I stepped onto the bus from out of nowhere came Ninja Auntie. She grabbed my waist and tried to pull me back but I was ready for her and I kicked out, catching her in the stomach and winding her. She let go of me and I screamed and ran onto the bus in tears. The bus took off and I didn't even look back, I just sat crying. I had got such a fright: at the age of eight I had predicted something that then happened. My cousin said, laughing, 'You got on the bus without paying.' And then they all carried on as if nothing had happened. I sat there very upset. Nothing more was said about the incident but the feelings from that day stayed with me for a long time. I was very shaken up. Nothing like that had ever happened to me before and I couldn't make any sense of it. Something I had thought about then played out for real. I never told anyone about the incident and my auntie never spoke to me about it. I was so pleased to see my lovely gran as I loved spending time with her and she really liked my company, so although I had been shocked following the incident, after an hour with my gran all was forgotten.

Sunday 1st January 2012

I had my grandchildren for a sleepover. They had me up at 7am. That's the thing about young children: they rise so early regardless of what time they go to bed! When one woke up, they would go to the other one's room to see if they were awake, and sometimes you'd hear little whispers as they discussed whether to come and wake you up. Then you'd see their little faces peer around the door to see if was safe to come in. They are so gorgeous, and I loved having them stay over at my house so much. I loved seeing their little tired faces in the morning with their eyes only half open as they came into my room still half asleep. They would squint and rub their little baby eyes as I put the television on, and the bright light came on. They would always jump into my bed for their morning cuddles and once we had their programmes on, I could take another half an hour to try and wake up whilst they watched *Peppa Pig*, or *Thomas the Tank Engine*. God, they made my heart melt. And even now they are much older, I still have those same protective feelings towards them.

It's a different type of love than that you have for your own children. When my own children would fall or hurt themselves, I would pick them up brush them down and make them feel better – I would never panic – but when my grandchildren hurt themselves or got upset, wow, the pain that ripped through me was something else. I couldn't let them cry as it hurt my heart too much. I just wanted them to be happy, safe and protected. I have been around my grandchildren and had them to stay since they were babies and I've always played a huge part in their lives. Those early years were very special and I had been so very lucky to spend so much time with them. To this day my grandchildren are at my door every day. We live on the same street so they come and go as if they have two homes, which I just love. We also have a special mum-proof cupboard, where we have lots of treats for them (and which mum doesn't know about.) That saying, 'when Mum says no ask Nana and, if all else fails, ask Grandma' (or in our case Nan 2) was written for my mum and me. We both find it very hard to say no to them!

Saturday 7th January 2012

I made an appointment to see my GP as I desperately needed some physio for my arm. It was getting ridiculous now – I had a very weak arm that didn't want to do anything. I was even struggling to hold a cup of tea. I couldn't help myself anymore as I didn't know what exercises I should be doing. The hospital physio had only shown me a few basic exercises to get the arm moving after surgery, and she had told me I would be followed up with physio as an out-patient, something that never happened. My GP was unimpressed that neither the consultant nor the hospital hadn't already organised physiotherapy for me and said it was unprofessional, so he referred me to my local hospital.

To try and get some normality back before I was 'poisoned' and wouldn't be able to spend as much time at the school, I decided to go there for what was supposed to be just a few hours. However, I ended up staying all day. It felt so good to be doing something I loved once again. I wasn't actually teaching dance, just managing the business, but this was what I did best. I loved speaking to all the parents and seeing the students, being busy and generally keeping my mind occupied. There were some lovely mums, who were now good friends and it was great see them all again. However, I paid the price for this: by the end of the day, my back was really sore. Because I had no muscle there anymore, this put a strain on my back whether I was sitting or walking, or doing anything really. My back felt like it was on fire – the pain was incredible. My body needed to adjust to the new me; I just wasn't sure how to do this. I had to take paracetamol throughout the day just to get me through, but I had been determined to stay at the dance school all day. It had been a good day with some positives and a few negatives:

1. It still hurt to sneeze. I had to hold my breast and back at the same time, and I appear to be coughing more, which was annoying (negative).

2. My armpit still smelt, perhaps not as bad as it did, but enough to make me gag. (Definitely negative).

3. My arm was not as swollen. The exercises must be working (positive).

4. It felt good to feel 'normal' tired. It was not tiredness from recovery, but from actually doing some work. I was mentally tired but this felt great – hello old life! (positive).

5. I could not lift anything heavy like the hoover or the washing (negative. Or was it?!)

6. I could not pole dance (I wasn't much good at that anyway).

7. I could not rock climb (really not bothered about this. Even if it were a matter of life or death, I'd be stuffed and would have to choose the latter option).

8. I had my first period since the operation (negative, I think. Who wants a period? Maybe those of you awaiting their period and hoping they're not pregnant may disagree!)

The dance school studios were in an old mill, which had been renovated and formed part of a business park. It was set in the grounds of an old chapel and its origins dated back to the 7th century. Sadly, inscriptions on headstones show there were many children buried within the grounds. We had researched the building's history following some strange activity within the school. Our studios were definitely haunted, and we felt it had to be a child's spirit due to some of the childish activity we had experienced. Maybe it was attracted to the children within the dance school. Anyway, we named our playful ghost 'Charlie'.

We have many stories from our days with Charlie, but one in particular stands out: it was a night in December and Jenna had been writing on the whiteboard in the reception area. She had knelt down as the white board was on a door and she was drawing holly leaves on it. I was hoovering in the corridor with Ryan and a door separated the corridor from where Jenna was in reception. It was nearly closing time and no one else was in the building but Jenna felt two little hands push hard into her back. She looked behind her, thinking it was either Ryan or me but there was no one there. She could hear the hoover so knew we were still in the corridor. She got up to check the toilet next to her, just in case one of us was tricking her but was surprised to see that the toilets were empty.

Jenna went back to writing on the board on her knees but once again felt two little hands push hard into her back. This time the push nearly knocked her over. She knew it was a child as she had clearly felt its small hands on her back. Ryan and I heard her scream from the corridor. I switched the hoover off and we ran through to reception expecting to see that she had had some kind of accident. She was sitting on the floor looking petrified.

'Did you just push me? It's not funny,' she said.

I said, 'No, we were in the corridor cleaning. What happened?'

Jenna told us what she'd felt and we knew this was Charlie messing around.

She asked, 'Are you sure it wasn't one of you trying to scare me?'

I assured her it wasn't: 'You would have heard the door opening if we'd come into reception,' I told her.

Poor Jenna was really shaken up. This was the first time Charlie had made any physical contact with any of us. The usual occurrence would be that we would close up the school at night, checking everything was in its place and the school was tidy and ready for the following day. We would check all the windows were locked and we always checked the trophy cabinet and behind the speakers in the studios for a specific reason.

When we would reopen the following day, we would notice that trophies and the teacher's belongings had been moved. We would find trophies and personal items hidden behind the big speaker in the studio. It was always behind one particular speaker that we would find things, so it became part of the process of closing and opening up to check to see what was hidden. It didn't happen every day; some days we would find the school just as we had left it the night before with everything in its place. We just never knew when it was going to happen and there never seemed to be any pattern to the moving and hiding of items.

The night before we were due to break up for Christmas, we were at the school setting up a raffle and gift stall ready for the next day. All the gifts on the stall had a raffle ticket stuck to them and the following day customers would choose a number from a bag. If their number matched any of the corresponding numbers attached to the gifts, they would win that prize. We also put selection boxes into Santa's sack ready for Santa to give them out to the children in the morning. All was quiet in the school and there was no sign of Charlie being present. All the other units within the business park had already closed for Christmas so we were the only ones in the building. In spite of this, we were never afraid. We never felt the energy was scary or threatening. When we had finished setting up for the morning, we locked the school and the rest of the building.

The following morning when we entered the school, we were shocked at what we found: the clock that sat on reception was now on the gift stall with a raffle ticket stuck to it. The gift that had been in its place was a child's memory keepsake box, which we found behind the speaker in the studio. Some of the selection boxes were out of Santa's bag and neatly placed on the floor of Santa's grotto. And where the clock usually sat, one of the gifts from the stall sat instead, still with its ticket attached. We had no idea how this had happened. Jenna and I were the only ones with a key to the school, and we had been there until late the previous night. We'd checked behind the speakers and made sure we had locked everything up when we left. Was this Charlie up to his old tricks again? We had no explanation.

Due to the increased activity we were experiencing we decided to approach someone we knew who had worked on a TV programme investigating paranormal activity. We arranged for them to spend a night in the dance school to see if they could come up with any answers. We also invited some of the teachers who had been on the receiving end of some of the playful activity. And because Jenna appeared to be the person to whom Charlie was most attracted, the team set up a Ouija board and asked Jenna to take the lead. This was the first time Jenna had tried anything like this. They explained to us what they were going to do and what to expect, and this is what followed:

- The investigator asked if anyone was there and the glass moved to 'yes'.
- Jenna took over and asked, 'Are you Charlie?' Again, the glass moved to 'yes'.
- Jenna asked, 'Is Charlie your real name?' The glass moved to 'no'.
- Jenna asked, 'Do you like us calling you Charlie?' The glass moved to 'yes'.

Jenna was so shocked she had tears in her eyes. She stood up as if she wanted to move away but kept her finger on the glass.

- Jenna asked if it was Charlie who kept playing tricks on us and the glass moved to 'yes' then spelt out the word PLAYING.

This was very unnerving. The conversation went on for some time before the team noticed that another entity had been attracted to the board. The conversation was now not as pleasant and caused some of those taking part to become anxious and they decided that they no longer wanted to participate. The investigating team decided it was a good time to end the activity and move outside of the school into the rest of the building to see what else they could detect. They spent many hours with their equipment going all over the old mill and yet the only time they picked anything up was when they were in the dance school. They agreed with us that it was a spirit of a child that was causing the activity and that it was probably attracted to the school as there were lots of children present. All the hiding and moving of objects was just a child playing or being mischievous.

One of our older students had arrived to join us later in the evening. She was late as she'd been for a spray tan, which was still a bit tacky and needed to dry. She had shorts on and kept her distance from us all. For most of the investigation we had been in the dark and at other times there had only been a small amount of light visible. So, it was only when the lights were switched on fully at the end of the investigation, we noticed she had a handprint from a very small child on her leg. It looked like a print from when children do hand painting, only this little handprint had been done on her fake tan! There was no explanation that we could give. The print was clear and on the front of her thigh, just the right height for a small child. The student was shocked at the idea that someone or something had touched her leg without her knowledge, particularly as there were no children in the building, or at least none that we could see!

It was nearly daybreak when the team began to wrap up. They agreed with us that we did indeed have a supernatural energy within the school, and they were confident it was a child entity. But even after receiving this confirmation, we still never felt afraid whilst at the school. And nothing changed following the investigation; things continued to get moved and we still found our trophies and various other items hidden behind the speaker. It was actually quite amusing as you never knew what you were going to find, and the idea that it was just a child playing meant we were OK with that. We had learnt to live with Charlie and we knew he wasn't going to cause us any harm. As the months passed, we began to hear knocks and whistles that would make us jump at times, but we knew it was just our Charlie, our dance school ghost.

Monday 9th January 2012

I received a letter today regarding the start date for commencing chemotherapy. It was to be Monday 30th January. I was actually quite excited about this as I wanted to prove the point that I was strong enough to win this battle, regardless of what poison they gave me. I was going into this battle with the same mentality of a pregnant woman whose birth plan is based on the fact that she thinks she's strong enough to cope with any pain, and therefore has made the decision to have a drug-free labour. I also believed I was strong enough to cope with any pain; I was determined I would hold onto my hair and nails, and I would get through this last hurdle (known as chemotherapy) problem free. But as we all know, many planned drug-free labours don't always go quite to plan, and women may find themselves reaching for the gas and air and begging the midwife for an epidural.

I thought I would cope with whatever chemotherapy threw at me and I thought my body would get through it naturally. I did however know that I would accept the following:

- anti-sickness for sickness.
- laxatives for constipation.
- steroids for helping my lungs and other vital organs.

And in fact, anything else they wanted to give me to help to combat the symptoms and make it a breeze. Well, there are no medals for trying to be a superhero, and if I had an army of medication on offer, I would accept it to make my side battle-ready. Bring on the chemo – I'm ready!

There was a lot of talk and worry about Poly Implants Protheses (PIP) which caused a global scare in 2012. The topic was all over the news. PIP implants were manufactured in France and were made from a cheaper industrial-grade silicone which had not been approved for medical use. The silicone gel was known to cause inflammation and possible scarring and was more prone to rupture than other implants. These implants caused a lot of worry over the possibility of other harmful long-term effects which were not yet known.

I checked with my consultant to make sure he had not used PIP implants on me, and was very relieved when he confirmed he hadn't. I am sure this was a worrying time for many. These implants had been used on so many women and for anyone who had the misfortune of having PIP implants, they would have to make the decision whether or not to have them removed. Ultimately, approximately 15,000 women made that decision.

I had always been very open about my cancer and never kept it a secret from anyone. I am very much an open book anyway and I was, and still am, happy to discuss my illness with anyone who wants to listen. Recently I was having my eyebrows tattooed and telling the woman carrying out the procedure all about it. Jenna was with me and the next minute I heard Jenna say, 'OK, the boob is out.'

Without even thinking, I had popped my boob out to show her how good it was.

She said, 'I don't know what I'm looking at!'

Exactly. The reconstruction is so good she couldn't

even tell I'd had it done. I really must stop popping the boob out though as it is becoming second nature. I don't even think about it most of the time – I just plop it out. One of these days it's going to get me into trouble!

As mentioned earlier, my frank and open conversations about cancer had helped another woman who had been too scared to get her lump checked out. If she had gone undiagnosed it could have had a different outcome. I would like to think that I helped in some small way to save her life.

If anyone reading my story has any fears about getting something checked out, whether it be a lump, or the fear of having a smear or anything else that might be worrying you, I urge you to see your doctor. Some things will not go away on their own – you just have to be brave and face your fears. Ignoring them could lead to an early death so please, if you have any concerns, get it checked out. Don't ever think you are wasting the doctor's time. If it turns out to be nothing sinister, great, and in fact doctors prefer this. But treatment is more successful if there is an early diagnosis of cancer. It is vital to treat it early to ensure a prompt return to health. The Be Clear on Cancer Campaign aims to improve early diagnosis of cancer by raising public awareness about symptoms of cancer and encouraging people to see their GP without delay. This campaign has worked really hard to spread the message that early diagnosis can save lives.

Wednesday 11th January 2012
There is always something …

My back was so sore again today and I was still on my period which, it occurred to me, could be my last period ever. And in fact, it turned out it *was* my last period ever;

the chemo stopped them for good and, along with the medication they put me on after the chemo, I was plunged into an induced menopause. God, this is a topic that deserves its own chapter and I will discuss this in detail later, but hot sweats, trouble sleeping, vaginal dryness (ouch) and weight gain are just a few of the symptoms of my menopause. I say 'my' as all woman experience menopause differently, so when I discuss mine it will be with the symptoms that *I* have experienced. But I am sure you'll all share my pain. Millions of women all over the world all trying to get through this horrible stage of life. You are not alone.

I decided to contact my GP and chase up why I had still not yet been referred for physio. I received a phone call from my doctor later that day who advised me that the local hospital would not accept me for physio as I had had my surgery carried out in the private sector, and therefore I should have my physio there as well. Were they for real? The doctor suggested I complain to the PCT (Primary Care Trust) so I phoned them and spoke to the receptionist who advised me that due to funding they couldn't accept me. They claimed that as I'd had my treatment privately, I was not entitled to get treatment on the NHS. This was ridiculous! I told her it was my choice whether I had surgery on the NHS or in the private sector and that I had actually *saved* the NHS money by paying personally for my cancer to be removed, (well with help from the Bank of Mum and Dad). I told her I did in fact try to get the surgery done on the NHS but my GP had advised me to go private so I had. Little did I know the amount of hassle this would subsequently cause. It seemed so unfair that I was being punished for saving the NHS money.

I asked, 'If I'd twisted my arm and gone to my GP for physio, I would have got it, so tell me what's so different about getting it now?'

But you know what it's like talking to a receptionist, they are the gate keepers of whatever they guard. They want to know what is wrong with you and insist on every little detail so they can decide who gets past them and who doesn't. They wield power like the doormen who think they're the FBI!

Getting nowhere, I changed tactic, threatening to go to the newspapers and tell them how an NHS nurse, who's just had major surgery and now needs physio, is getting turned away. If I couldn't get my arm working again, I couldn't nurse. I would tell them that the NHS refused to give me a breast support nurse (I'd forgotten about that – they said I had to use the breast support nurse from the hospital where I had my surgery) and now refused me physio even though they were giving me chemotherapy. How could they accept me for one but not the other? There was no rationale. To leave a cancer patient with no support was disgusting. The hospital had had so much bad press of late, I suggested, yet another negative story could be very damaging. All I was asking for was one appointment so I could learn to do my exercises properly. I wasn't going to let it go, I warned her, so advised her to get it sorted out.

I was furious but it worked. Ten minutes later she phoned me back and said the GP needed to send the referral to the hospital once again. Although physio was not something they should do (what absolute bollocks), they would sort something out for me. How bloody generous when I had saved them £10,000 the cheeky bastards!

Oh, I forgot to mention that the consultant who carried out my surgery worked for free (though not free for me); he donated the £10,000 I paid to the Poppy Appeal, which was nice. He even checked with me first to make sure I was happy with his decision, which of course I was. I was happy to be helping any charity out and thought my consultant was a very honourable and privileged person to be able to work for free and support such a wonderful charity. Apparently, he would choose a different charity each time he carried out his private work. So, as well as saving the NHS money, I had also helped the Poppy Appeal.

I received another strange phone call the same day from my consultant saying, 'Good news: we sent your biopsy off for a second opinion and the results show you do not have triple negative cancer after all!'

Can you believe this? I was stunned. (This was becoming a habit – me being lost for words!) It turned out that my cancer had been using my oestrogen to grow, but only by 30%. This meant that I had a cancer which needed oestrogen to grow. Usually this type of cancer will show a positive result of 80%, but as mine was only showing 30% they said it was a rarer form. Anyway, this was great news! I was constantly being caught off guard and I was up and down depending on what they told me. This was why I would have to be on Tamoxifen – this medication would stop me producing oestrogen. Thank God they found this out when they did, as the chemotherapy they give you is specific to the type of cancer you have.

I started to think, wait, are you sure I even *had* cancer? How can you get the results wrong, and why did you feel the need for a second opinion? Something must have triggered them to seek one, but what? Anyway, thank God they did! These are questions that I would never get the answer to, like some of life's true mysteries: where is the Bermuda triangle? Did Elvis really die on the toilet? Did man really land on the Moon? And who was Jack the Ripper? Why did my mammogram show a negative result when it should have shown a positive one? And why did they seek a second opinion on my biopsy? There are just no answers!

To top my day off I had another phone call, this time from the private hospital to let me know I still owed them £800 for the mammogram and scan treatment, for which I thought I had already paid. Apparently, I was given the wrong price (which was bloody convenient). Now I had my new boob I could hardly give it back, so I had no choice but to pay. I had already discussed this bill with my consultant when they had sent me another invoice, and he had told me in no uncertain terms not to pay it. He said I'd had a package deal, (like an all-inclusive holiday but without the glamour!) for which I had already paid in full so I must ignore it. I had been quoted a price and all my care and scans were supposed to be included, but now apparently, I had to pay for extras.

You think you have done well when you pay for your all-inclusive holiday, then you find out when you get there that to be able to get a half-decent drink you have to pay extra, or continue drinking the watered-down alcohol that is included for the rest of the holiday. I phoned my consultant to double check but he had changed his tune and now urged me to pay it. So much for his original advice! I should have recorded what he said as he tended to change his mind at the drop of a hat. He couldn't seem to remember what he told you from one day to the next. My advice? Always get your quotes in writing for anything, including car insurance, home insurance, work from tradesmen and your surgery!

I had to phone the bank to let them know about my chemo and to give permission for Jed to act on my behalf. The woman on the other end of the line said, 'Oh, I see you're a nurse. While I have you on the line, can you please just help me? I have this rash and it's red and sore – what do you think it is?'

As nurses, we get this a lot. How people can think you can diagnose a rash over the phone is beyond me!

After spending most of the day on the phone, my final call was from the private hospital saying my local hospital had no physio appointments available so I had been referred to them. I was to start on Wednesday 18th January at 7pm. A good end to my day – phew! But why did I have to fight for everything? I told you there was always something. Why was nothing ever straight forward? At least the private hospital was nice, and I felt OK going there so I was happy about that. All's well that ends well!

Monday 16th January 2012

Today I had my first appointment to meet my new consultant at my local hospital and he seemed to be very nice. He was very impressed with my new boob and asked me who had performed the surgery. He said my consultant had done a great job and added that he'd never seen any surgery as good as this and that my consultant had produced a better outcome than he could ever have achieved.

Wow! That was some compliment. And I was so glad I had been guided down the private health care path where, not only had I met the most wonderful consultant and surgeon, but I had also received the best reconstruction, something I was over the moon with.

I have to say that whenever I had a check-up with my surgeon, he would always bring a nurse into the room and, whilst I was sitting with my boobs hanging out, say, 'What do you think of that?'

The nurse would stare at my boobs, wondering what response to give and he would add, 'It's a mastectomy and reconstruction. How good is that?'

He was so proud of his work. No wonder I always had my boob out! I was just as proud as he was and wanted to shout from the rooftops that the old-style mastectomy was long gone. There was no longer any need to be afraid of having a mastectomy. You could look just as good (and normal) following a mastectomy and reconstructive surgery – my beautiful boob proves that. Though it did make me question why, when I had my first consultation, my surgeon had thought it necessary to show me photos of mastectomies that didn't look anything like the results he was achieving. If I had seen a photo of my reconstruction instead, my stress levels would have been halved going into the operation; I would have gone into surgery feeling a lot happier than I did at the time!

So, my new consultant didn't have my notes (here we go again …) so was unable to discuss much about my operation or the results. He said once he knew more, he would let me know, but in the meantime, he didn't want to speculate and get anything wrong. He gave me another appointment for Tuesday 24th January to have my new-patient talk about chemo with the nurse and said the treatment would start on the 30th January.

Although this was annoying, I could understand him not wanting to give me incorrect information. And I remembered an incident with a doctor on the ward I once worked on: he was looking at a patient's notes and had put his chest X-ray on the light box. He said, 'Yes, he has a chest infection' and drew up some antibiotics for him. The elderly gentleman had his first dose of antibiotics before the doctor realised that the notes he had read were not actually this gentleman's notes at all, and the chest X-ray was not of his chest. The doctor in question looked at me and said, 'Well, antibiotics never hurt anyone, it will do him no harm.'!

As I left the unit, I picked up a leaflet on how to lose weight following cancer treatment. It was a study and I decided to phone them to find out more. When I phoned them however, they said the study was a year old and no longer available –the leaflets should have been removed from the unit. Typical!

Wednesday 18th January 2012

Following my referral, I had my first physio session at the hospital. The appointment was for 7pm and as you're aware, I am always a little tired by this time. However, it was very helpful and the physio was really nice. The physio explained that the skin was made up of layers like an onion and that, in my case, the layers of the onion had been cut (funny how they describe everything as food. My lump was a pea!). She gave me a little massage over the scar to loosen up the scar tissue, showed me exercises to do at home and then gave me another appointment for three weeks' time. That was all I had wanted. Now I knew what exercises I was supposed to do, I could get on with strengthening my arm and getting my mobility back. The physio said I needed physiotherapy, otherwise the scar tissue would become tight and I would lose mobility in that arm for good. She also told me that lack of exercise can cause lymphedema in an arm where lymph nodes had been removed. And so, physio was to play an important part in my recovery and mobility – and the NHS had wanted to refuse this part of my treatment!

24th January 2012

Difficult Conversations

Wow! I thought having the conversation about surgery was bad enough but the conversation with the nurse who would be giving me chemotherapy (chemo) was so much worse. Mum and Jed were with me and it was *not* what I had been expecting.

She told me all about my first chemo and said that there would be a nasty taste and smell; I would feel the liquid going through my veins and then it would hit me between my legs (in my vagina) like a prickly sensation. OK … I could cope with that – it didn't sound too bad. She wouldn't discuss any further sessions because she said we must take each step of chemo at a time. We should concentrate on each dose and she would explain what to expect with each new one when I was due to receive it.

There were to be six sessions over six months. The first three were to be a different cocktail to the last three.

The two different types of chemo attack the cells at different stages. The nurse said she would discuss the side effects for the last three doses when the time was right – now was not the right time. Then she said, 'We need to discuss losing your hair.'

NO WAY! I am not having this conversation. I was desperate to just run away and cry, but I didn't want to cry in front of anyone and I couldn't really run away. It was becoming real. But I was NOT losing my hair.

I said, 'I don't want to discuss it,' but she said, 'You have to, and you have to face up to what is going to happen with your hair. It is going to happen, so we have to discuss it.'

OMG, I felt sick. As daft as it sounded, this felt like the worst conversation I had had during the journey so far. Looking back, I see how trivial it was, but at the time I was so vulnerable and I felt like my whole world was collapsing in on me.

She told me it would be approximately eleven days after my first chemo that I would start to lose my hair.

WTF! I felt my breath being snatched away again and I thought I was going to pass out. I thought I would have had a few months to be able to get used to the idea, but no, I had just eleven days! This was just awful and, for me, one of the worst parts of the whole journey. To anyone reading this, you may think 'it's only hair – look what you've gone through already', but unless you ever find yourself in this situation (and I hope you never do), you can never fully understand just how bad it feels. (In hindsight, it was nowhere near as bad as I thought. In fact, I looked quite gorgeous without hair!)

Anyway, back to this awful situation ... I had to discuss my hair loss and my options and I felt like a child again: with my head down and using every ounce of my strength not to break down, I sat and pretended to listen to what she was saying.

Do you remember when your mum would drag you to the dentist and you'd be so scared not wanting the treatment? Well, that's how I felt. She gave me a number to call to have a wig fitted in Manchester, even though I didn't want one, and I left the hospital very deflated. No one knew what to say to me to make it all right and I couldn't discuss with anyone just how bad I felt.

Mum kept saying, 'It'll be fine, and your hair will grow back,' but nothing anyone could say helped me at that time. We even went to the health shop to see if we could get some vitamins to strengthen my hair and nails before the chemo started. I got hair nets and grips from the dance school so I could protect my hair. My master plan was to wrap lots of hair nets around the hair to protect it and to use hair grips and spray to make it so solid it couldn't move and fall out. I could see the logic in this and I really thought it would work. The nurse had told me I would wake up each day and there would be hair on my pillow. She said, 'Don't look at it – get Jed to clean it up each morning'.

Really? Was I going to lose so much each day that Jed would have to clean it up? OMG I was not expecting this, I really didn't want it to happen. Imagine being told that next week you will lose your hair. It was all so surreal. I just wanted it all to go away. When I was a child, my mum could make everything all right again. Not now, not today or next week. This was something none of us could prevent from happening. I felt so out of control again. But I would not let my hair go not without a fight!

I was offered a 'cold cap', which is a painful cap that goes on your head and freezes the hair root so the chemo does not attack the head area as much, meaning you lose only a small amount of hair, making your hair a lot thinner rather than going completely bald. But it's apparently a painful procedure and makes the whole chemo process a lot longer. I declined it as I wanted the chemo to get every cell in my body; I didn't want any left behind. So as scared and upset as I was about losing my hair, I knew this was the right thing going forward.

Today had been the worst shopping trip I had ever been on and I would not be repeating it ever again. We went to Manchester to look at wigs. Never in my life did I think I would have to go wig shopping! Jenna and my mum came with me. It was a horrible shop in a back street in Manchester, and we were shown in and sat in a little room. It all looked so stuffy and old fashioned. The shop reminded me of the one in Diagon Alley from the Harry Potter films, where he got his wand from. It wouldn't have looked out of place in a museum!

A very stuffy older lady told me to sit on the chair in front of the mirror and then began the process of offering me various wigs to try on, all of which looked absolutely ridiculous. I had to choose one though as it was free. I felt awful looking in the mirror with a wig on. The woman said, 'Try to imagine when you have no hair how it will sit on your head. It only looks strange because you have hair.'

Don't say it looks strange because I have hair; I look normal because I have hair. Show me some compassion, woman! Your wigs are old fashioned and look ridiculous on me for that reason – do *not* blame my beautiful hair!

She brought out a tan-coloured wig cap to hide my hair so I could see what it would be like to be bald and get an idea of how the wig would actually sit on my head. It took all my strength to look at myself in the mirror. I didn't look like me anymore and, worse still, none of the wigs suited me, even though Mum and Jenna said they looked nice (they didn't). I didn't feel nice wearing it and I knew I would never wear it. It was far too dark for my complexion and was a peculiar shape. I left the shop feeling even more deflated than I had when I first entered. They could at least have had some younger people working there and some trendier wigs for us younger cancer victims. This was the worst shopping trip ever!

When we came out of the shop (back into the 21st century) we went into a nearby hotel and ordered a hot chocolate. It was strange going from a dark old-fashioned dingy shop into a smart modern hotel. The contrast couldn't have been greater.

It was a cold day in January and the sky was overcast with dark menacing clouds. It was nice to sip the sweet hot chocolate, which warmed me up immediately. We sat by the window watching the world go by. People were going about their everyday lives, all wrapped up in their winter coats trying to keep some protection against the elements. Everyone was in their own little bubble and all had some place to be. There was so much hustle and bustle with everyone rushing about. I felt as though I was in one of those adverts where the person with cancer stands still and the rest of the world goes on around them. That's an accurate representation of how I felt in that moment. I sat quietly drinking my hot chocolate and made the conscious decision that I would definitely not need the wig; I would NOT be losing my hair!

Chemotherapy

In this part of my story there are days where we do not say so much. Most days blended into each other. What can you say when you are so ill and feeling on the brink of death? My mum was back from Spain to help me during this time and was keeping a record of my days for me. A lot of the days blended into one with pain and sickness and me in bed unable to do anything. Anyway, here goes …

Monday 30th January 2012

Mum

1.30pm: Carolann received her first dose of chemo. She was very nervous but just wanted to get it started. The taste and smell hit her straight away just like they said it would.

My First Chemo

Today was my first day of chemo treatment and the start of the next chapter of my cancer journey. Jed came with me and I have to say I was rather nervous. They put me in a cubicle, but I could see the other patients all hooked up to their chemo cocktails. I was not expecting this. I liked my privacy and had thought I would be behind a curtain for my treatment, but no, it appears chemo patients like to talk to each other, which is fine, but as you will know by now, when I'm nervous, I just like to be quiet. Plus, by now I was used to private treatment and liked being treated like the lady of the manor or 'Lady Muck' as Jed called me.

The other patients were all friendly, they were also bald and proud and some had little caps or scarves on their heads. I still didn't want to speak to them though and I didn't want to see their bald heads as it scared me shitless. I was in no mood to make small talk, so I asked if I could have the curtain pulled around me. To get through this I needed to be quiet and in my own little world. I know I sound unsociable, and I admit I was very unsociable, but this was the only way I could cope with any stress. I was still coming to terms with this new way of life and the people who now surrounded me, and I wasn't yet ready to be part of this group.

It hurt when the nurse put the canula in. They said they would continue to use the same arm and vein for as long as they could. They couldn't use my other arm due to the surgery. If my veins were to collapse on the arm they were using, they could insert something called a chemo port into my chest which would get left in place for the duration of my chemo. They could then use this for access instead of a vein. Nope, I didn't want that either. That definitely would not be happening! To be fair, my veins were pretty good and I knew they wouldn't let me down.

So, the chemo hit my veins and just like the poison it is known to be, it lived up to its name. It tasted and smelt disgusting, like a very potent chemical. My mouth and throat took the full force from it immediately. As it hit my throat, I felt like I'd been winded, and it caught me off guard. It was like someone had punched me in the throat. Then it hit my nose and I had to rub it as it became very itchy and irritated. I could feel the chemical poison race through my veins and around my body, eager to start raging its war against my cells. I felt it travel right through me – it was such a strange feeling. Then it hit my vagina. Wow! I felt like I was sitting on a prickly pear. I can't even describe it how itchy it was; I wanted to jump up and rub it, but you can't jump up and rub your fanny in public! And that was it: the chemo was now in my system and I had to sit there for a couple of hours whilst my body filled up with more of this chemical poison.

Little did I know that the awful smell and taste – even the words associated with the smell and taste – would stay with me forever. It was years before I could even speak about chemo without gagging, and even to this day, certain smells and tastes affect me. I even feel sick just writing about it. This is a truly nasty experience for anyone to have to go through but again, your body will learn to help you forget the trauma of being poisoned, though not completely as I have just discovered writing this!

I actually felt OK after the first dose and left the hospital wondering if that was it. Maybe I was just strong so it wouldn't bother me. If only I'd known what was round the corner. I popped up to see my parents and my dad said, 'You look really well – I was expecting you to look ill.'

Give it time Dad, give it time!

Tuesday 31st January

Mum

Carolann was very ill today. She was aching all over and felt very sick. Her urine was a bright red colour which they had told her to expect.

Wednesday 1st Feb– Saturday 4th Feb

Carolann was so poorly she didn't know what to do with herself. She couldn't drink anything and she hated the taste of water. She was aching all over and was very ill. She just lay in bed or on the settee. I was so worried about her.

Tuesday 7th Feb

Carolann was still in bed poorly and unable to do anything. I made her boiled ribs and cabbage. Today she was craving a Gregg's iced finger, so we made sure she had a couple in at all times.

Wednesday 8th Feb–Monday 13th Feb

Carolann kept thinking about her hair coming out. It was terrible seeing her like this. She was so weak, and her bones were aching. She just lay in her bed or on the settee. She kept thinking about next Monday when she would get her next dose. She has not recovered from the first dose yet and the next one is looming.

Tuesday 14th–Sunday 19th Feb

She was still not well but was starting to pick up a bit. She was being so brave and positive but talking all the time about losing her hair. She was so tired and sore, but her positivity was great.

I'm back! Well, what a horrible ride that was! I was not expecting that at all. By day two I was so ill and when I say ill, I mean ILL. I was passing red urine, which they said I would, I felt so sick and the pain – WOW is all I can say. It was like someone taking a hammer to my joints and smashing them over and over; I felt the initial blow each time. And the taste in my mouth was like dirty drain water (not that I had ever tasted dirty drain water, but I could imagine its thick, grey, sludgy taste). It makes me gag just writing about it. Everything, especially water was absolutely disgusting. I had just picked up a bit when I was due my next dose. I was not looking forward to this. God help me, was all I could say.

Monday 20th Feb: Second Chemo day

Mum

1.30pm I attended the hospital with Carolann for her second dose of chemo. She had to see the nurse first to make sure she was well enough to get her next dose. She was, and once again the chemo hit her straight away, making her nose itch badly and the taste was horrible again. These side effects are due to the chemicals in the chemo. We are going to call this day one.

Losing my hair

Tuesday 21st Feb Day 2

Mum

This was quite a good day. She had kept occupied doing things for the dance school show, costumes etc. Her hair is coming out bit by bit but we won't discuss that with her.

So, back to my hair. I do not recall the dates as I have only photos to show my hair's downfall but I now had my hair tied up and fastened tight to my head. I had three hair nets wrapped around it and loads of grips to keep the hair in place. Day 11 had come and gone, I was about to have my next dose of chemo and I still had my hair. I told you I would keep it, well some of it! I knew this could be beaten!

I was losing bits of hair but still holding onto the majority of it. I was doing everything in my power to hold on to it for as long as I could. The nurse at the hospital had laughed and said she had never seen anything like it. She couldn't believe I'd managed to keep my hair for this long. I was wearing a little cotton cap at night and each morning Jed would empty it, so I didn't have to see how much hair I was actually losing. Really, by this stage I should have been bald. However, I was aware of a little bald patch at the back of my head – I could feel it – so I asked Jed to take a photograph. He said, 'Are you sure you want to see it?'

Yes, I did want to see it although when I looked at the photo I nearly cried. The back of my head had lots of little bald patches. It was a great shock to me. I wasn't expecting this even though I'd been warned. For some reason when the nurse told me I was going to lose my hair, I didn't think I actually would! No one wants to see bald patches on their head. I wanted to cry but I kept it together and remained strong.

Each morning there was more and more hair falling out. I had to be careful; if I moved a strand of hair, it would just pull out straight from the root with no force. It was very strange, and I tried not to touch my hair to prevent more loss. As well as the large amounts in the cap, which I wore every night, there was also a lot of hair on my pillow. I tried not to look and Jed would try and clear away as much as possible. I still had the mass of hair on top of my head, held in place by hairnets and grips, but it now resembled a bird's nest. The rest of my head was now nearly bald and I looked very strange with just a mass of matted hair on the top of my head. Still, I would not be beaten, and I would hold on to this matted hair for as long as I could. My head was really itchy, and I could pop my fingers underneath the mass of hair, lift it up and scratch my head (which was also now bald), then put it back down again. It would have made make a great comedy sketch!

I said I wouldn't wear a wig and yet my own hair now looked more like a wig than an actual wig would have! I was so stubborn and so determined to prove that you can keep your hair whilst having chemo. If I'd gone out in the wind this mass of hair on top of my head would have blown off! In fact, you know what it looked like; you know those brown material liners you put in hanging baskets? Well, like them only a lot thicker, and after the birds have tried to pull strands out for their nests!

This mass of hair was making me uncomfortable though and when I looked in the mirror, I noticed that when I put my fingers under it to scratch, the hair was only held on by a few strands and by that, I mean no more than about six! To all intents and purposes, it was a wig, only held on by a few hairs. I had to come to terms with the fact that all I had managed to do was hold on to a clump of matted hair yet my head underneath was actually bald. So, I made the difficult decision to remove the mass. All I had to do was lift it up and the few strands keeping it attached came away easily. I didn't even have to cut them, they just pulled out. So, there you have it: I was bald. I didn't win my hair battle after all, but I certainly gave it a good fight and held on to my hair for longer than anyone imagined.

To this day I still have the mass of hair – I keep it in a carrier bag, and the hair nets and hair grips are still matted into it. I have to say it was such a relief to get it off as my head was getting sore, itchy and uncomfortable. And ultimately, it had been my choice to remove the hair, not cancer's or the chemo and that was the difference. I could have left it on for a bit longer but I chose to remove it as it was hot and itchy and my scalp was getting little bits of cradle cap. I was left with just a few strands of hair on my head, but I had a nicely shaped head so this wasn't as bad as I thought it would be. I felt instant relief getting rid of the hot itchy mass and I was adamant I wouldn't wear a wig; I would continue to wear caps and head scarves. There are so many nice head pieces to choose from, so I spoiled myself and spent over £100 on new head wear!

I remember the first time I went out with my cap on: we had gone to Asda and I had been so worried about being out with no hair and just my cap on. I felt like everyone would be watching me. I'm sure this wasn't the case, but I did notice some people had a second glance. I am sure people look and assume you have cancer, but actually, I didn't have cancer anymore.

Anyway, I coped with the outing and became used to being out and about with my cap on. But I will always remember the feelings of anxiety I experienced that first time. Considering I'm a very outgoing bubbly person (I'm a Gemini) this initial outing made me temporarily lose my confidence and left me feeling very vulnerable. There was no blending in with the crowd on that day.

We had been very open with the grandchildren regarding both my hair loss and treatment. They knew I was now bald, and they were OK with this. They were only five and six but understood that Nana got tired easily, and they were so well behaved, bless them. They were really gentle with me to ensure they never hurt me on my surgery site.

My granddaughter was playing with her Lego figures and removed the plastic hair from one of the figures. She said to her mum, 'Look mummy – it's Nana.'

I thought this was quite clever for a five-year-old!

We decided to play a little trick on them so I put on my wig, which they had not yet seen, (it had never been out of the box since the day I got it) and when they came into the room I said, 'Look, my hair has grown back!'

Their little innocent faces were a picture as they said excitedly, 'Look Nana's hair's grown back!' They had only seen me a few days previously and I had been bald then. They had no concept of the time required for hair to grow back. Then I pretended I was going to sneeze: 'Ah ah ah … choooo!' I whipped the wig off and threw it on the floor. They both looked so shocked – their nana had just sneezed and her hair fell off. When they realised what I had done they fell about laughing, both taking turns to put the wig on. At least the bloody horrible thing was getting some use!

Wednesday 22nd February: Day 3

Mum
What a bad day Carolann had today. She felt so sick and every bone in her body was hurting her.

Thursday 23rd February: Day 4

Carolann had been in agony all day today. Every bone was hurting her. She was so tired and sick. My poor little girl alone in the house all day. I had been warned to stay away from her until I had finished my antibiotics for shingles as I was told it could make her seriously ill. What a situation for her. She wanted strawberry milk to drink so I went and got her some, put it in the kitchen, washed the bottle and cleaned all the door handles with antiseptic wipes so she didn't catch anything from me. I couldn't go upstairs to see her in case I passed the infection on. Carolann fancied something different to eat or drink each day and we did everything we could to ensure she got what she wanted. However, some of her requests were becoming more difficult to fulfil!

Friday 24th February: Day 5

Another day of pain for my girl. She was so tired that she couldn't even get out of bed. She was sleeping the day away alone in the house. I just kept sending her texts and praying for her. She could not eat as she had a very sore mouth and was struggling to drink as everything tasted so horrible to her.

Saturday 25th February: Day 6

Carolann said the pain was less today but she still couldn't eat or drink. She was so weak she could hardly walk and had to stay in bed all day. My poor baby. Again, I didn't see her because of my infection so could only send messages to her. She wasn't up for talking as she was so weak and her mouth hurt.

Sunday 26th February: Day 7

She was still really weak and could hardly walk. She managed to get downstairs by sitting on her bottom so that she could lie on the settee. (She was too weak and sore to stand). That was a good sign though and meant she had picked up a bit.

Chemo pain and symptoms

This dose of chemo I was having was absolutely bloody awful. I had such a great pain threshold normally, but this pain was the worst I had ever experienced. This must be what it feels like to be tortured. As I've already said, it felt like someone had taken a hammer to my hands, especially one finger on my right hand, the one next to my thumb. It felt like it was being hit with a hammer, then seconds later I felt the same pain, and again and again, all night long. Then the same thing would happen in my ankle. I didn't know what part of my body to hold next. I was rocking in my bed holding my painful joints and moaning like I was in labour. This was the only thing I could think of doing. Then I would shout, 'Ow!' each time the pain got worse. Nothing helped to ease it and I wasn't sure how I was going to get through it. It was exhausting and I couldn't sleep because of it. There were no words to describe it and no end in sight.

This was a very low moment in my life. Lying in the dark with the worst pain in the world, I felt very alone. These are just some of the symptoms I experienced:

- Excruciating pain in every joint
- Sickness & vomiting
- Exhaustion
- Breathlessness
- Weight gain (especially your belly – something they call 'chemo belly' – and face due to steroids)
- No taste (apart from chemo)
- No smell (apart from chemo)
- Unable to walk
- Rash
- Skin peeling
- Ulcers in your mouth
- Sore throat
- Indigestion

- Heart burn
- Hair loss
- Nail damage
- Depression

Before having chemo, they had made me sign a consent form to say that I understood that having this treatment could lead to my death. Never in my life did I think I would have to sign something that included those words. Ordinarily, if something had a chance to cause death you would stay well away from it. But what choice did I have? It was either take a chance with chemo and hopefully kill the cancer or take the chance that the surgery had completely eradicated it.

I was now so weak I was unable to walk. I was like a little old lady. Ryan and Jed took an arm each to support me, and I shuffled from my bedroom to the bathroom, having to rest when I got to the bedroom door because I was so breathless. I could hardly lift my feet; the effort was too much and my feet hurt so badly. I only wanted to go to the toilet and, for this brief moment, I looked at both Ryan and Jed having to take me to the toilet at the age of 42 and I wanted to cry. What had I become? I was trying so hard to win this fight but by God, it is wasn't easy. And as strong as I normally was, this was proving to be the biggest challenge of my life and a battle I felt I was losing at that point.

When Jenna came to see me, I was so unwell, and I didn't think I could take the pain much longer. It was so severe, and I felt so weak and sick. I just wanted to curl up and cry, but I couldn't even do that. I told Jenna if I ever got cancer again, I would not have chemotherapy. I would rather die than go through this torture again. And much as I hate to admit it, at that time death appeared an easier option for me; one that would remove the pain and give me some release. I could see no end in sight and after days of excruciating pain and sickness, I was exhausted with nothing left to give. Frankly, this chemo was a big bastard and just too powerful for me to take on.

Looking back, this was the one and only time I became this low and I can now see how drastically chemo affected not just my body, but my mind. Of *course*, I would ALWAYS fight to save my life and, looking back, I see what a silly thing this was to say, but it shows what frame of mind I was in at that time. It has taken me years to forget the pain enough to be able to move on. In fact, I will never completely forget but if I had to fight again (which I won't) but if I *had* to, I would.

Making you forget a trauma is the body's way of protecting itself. When you give birth you say, never again, but then you go back and do it all over again. If we didn't have this mechanism, we would only ever have one child. Though I have to say I would rather give birth a thousand times over with no pain relief than go through chemo again.

Tuesday 28th February: Day 9
Mum

Today Carolann was craving tomato soup. This was an easy one to fulfil. She managed to eat a little of the soup and have some melon. She has had a heavy bleed for a week now and is losing a lot of blood today. She's worried as her periods had stopped due to the chemo so she is not sure what this bleeding could be. She rang the doctors and they are sending a nurse to take a blood sample from her.

Thursday 2nd March: Day 11

Carolann phoned me at 9.30am. The consultant had just phoned her to give her the good news 'a positive diagnosis' about her future. We are all so happy for her! Carolann is very ill today. She has a headache and the thought of more chemo is making her sick. The last episode was so severe, she doesn't think she can cope with it again. We went to the hospital for her physio. She is yawning all the time and is tired and depressed. When she got home, she went straight upstairs to bed. It is all too much for her. My poor little baby girl.

Friday 9th March: Day 19

We went to the hospital for her blood test results. The nurse said that Carolann might be suffering from too much chemo, and that it might not be a good idea to have her next dose on Monday. Carolann felt better straight away at this news. They think her cells are saturated with chemo and this is why is she is not recovering well in between doses.

So, they told me originally that the chemo would flatten me for three weeks and then I would have a week to recover before the next dose. However, I only managed to get a day or two at the end of the fourth week before they poisoned me again. I wasn't getting a break from the symptoms and I had no recovery time, consequently, I felt unwell all the time. When I spoke to the nurse, she explained that all my cells were so saturated with the chemo (I had so much of it in my system) they were not getting a chance to fully recover before I was given my next dose. The cycle would then start all over again, but my cells were still saturated from the previous dose. Because of this, I may be given a break from the next dose to allow my body to recover – yeah!

Every time I got to my recovery day, (which was always a Sunday) I tried to make the most of it. That one day a month I would go out shopping, just wandering around town trying to feel normal again. I never wanted the shops to close as I didn't want the day to be over. Once everywhere closed it was time to go home and then the next day was chemo day, back in bed feeling unwell again. And now I knew what to expect it was even worse. But this last day, before my chemo restarted, was always the best. I would feel back to some sort of normality and I just wanted to be out for as long as I could, no matter how tired I became. I didn't want the day to end but as it was a Sunday, it always ended prematurely as the shops closed early! Once I got back in the car to head home, I knew that was it for another three weeks. However, there may be some hope as I may not have to have it the following day as they weren't expecting my blood results to be good. We would see …

I was sitting in bed this morning, eating my porridge, watching the telly and generally minding my own business. It was a beautiful morning so I had the curtains open and the blinds pulled back. I was not yet dressed and wore just my bra. My cap was off so my bald head could get some air around it. I had no eyebrows and no eye lashes, so I looked very strange, especially with a few strands of hair sprouting from my head. I was just putting a spoonful of porridge into my mouth when I heard a noise. When I looked to see what it was, there was the bloody window cleaner, who was clearly not expecting to see me naked and bald! For a brief moment we made eye contact and it was clear neither of us knew what to do next. I decided to act casual (like you do), so with my mouth still open and my spoonful of porridge en-route into it, I pretended I couldn't see him and carried on eating. In turn, he continued to clean the bedroom window whist I sat and ate. Gradually, and discreetly, I pulled the quilt over my boobs, so by the time the window was clean all he could see was my bald head. He played the same game, pretending he couldn't see me through the glass. What must he have thought? It was a big window and he didn't rush, but I suppose he didn't have to, seeing as neither of us could see the other!

Halfway There

Monday 12th March
Mum

Chemo Day! This will be the third session if Carolann has it, and she will be then be halfway through her treatment.

1.30pm Carolann went into hospital happy today as she wasn't expecting to have her chemo. However, unexpectedly, her blood results were good, so the consultant advised her to have it. Postponing it could have an effect on her recovery and would mean the end date is also pushed back. So, the decision was made to go ahead. We had to wait until 4pm though as there were no anti-sickness tablets for her to take. She had her chemo and experienced all the same nasty sensations as before.

Tuesday 13th March: Day 1

We will call this day one. Carolann was better this time than on the other 'day ones'. She was in bed watching daytime TV. In the afternoon she came over to Jenna's house but only for fifteen minutes. It was a lovely sunny day. She is weak in body but still strong in mind as she walked around the garden then sat in the shade for a little while. She couldn't stay long as she was just not well enough. I watched as my lovely daughter slowly walked back to her own house wearing her hat. Please God, our Lady and Saint Ann, please please make her better soon.

Jed
Today Carolann requested I get her spicy crisps. She has no taste buds and is desperate to be able to taste something. I went to every supermarket and shop and spent £20 on crisps and snacks. She opened every bag and tasted each snack. She would have one crisp and say, 'No, I can't taste it', then open the next bag. She did this until she had tasted all the snacks I'd bought. She realised that her sense of taste had completely gone – she was unable to taste any flavours at all – and she was very disappointed.

Having no taste buds was driving me mad and each day I would crave something new. My family were great for trying to fulfil my needs, but everything just tasted the same – like dirty drain water. Poor Jed spent £20 trying to find me a spicy snack I could taste but his efforts were wasted; I could not taste any of them.

Thursday 15th March: Day 3
Mum
Carolann sent me a text asking me to come and see her. She was feeling sick and tired and I helped her into the bath. She spent the rest of the day in bed. She was thinking about Spain, wanting to have ice cream from the ice-cream parlour at the top of the road by our Spanish house. She also wanted crispy duck and seaweed.

My daughter is hungry. Her symptoms are slow to kick in this time. I am so worried about her. It is not fair; she is so good. I would not hesitate to change places with her.

Friday 16th March: Day 4

This was a really bad day for her: the symptoms may have been slow to kick in but now they have kicked in with a vengeance. She has been shivering hot and cold all night. Her bones ache, and her face swollen and red. She had sickness all day and was so weak and depressed. I stayed with her all day. At 4pm she had cravings for food, but it's food she is not supposed to have with chemo. She fancies Marks and Spencer's cottage cheese and noodles. Jenna went straight out to buy it for her mum. Poor Jenna; she says nothing but keeps it all bottled up inside her.

Saturday 17th March: Day 5

Poor Carolann: her tongue is full of bacteria. She can't eat, drink or swallow. Her bones ache and she's nauseous, depressed, weak and very ill. She's been in bed all day with gastric problems, sickness, and pain. I cannot say anything to cheer her up or do anything to help her. Please God, Our Lady and Saint Ann, please help her. She has a lump on the back of her neck. We are all so worried.

Friday 23rd March: Day 11

Carolann said today is the first time since 11th November 2011 that she had felt 'normal'. How good was that? This is the best news I've had in months! She was full of life today. She was wearing a navy-blue turban, and she looked beautiful. She had even manged to put her washing out – a great achievement for her. Carolann does not have a lot of energy but she keeps doing things in between resting – good on her. My little fighter. She is full of positivity.

A New Poison

Monday 2nd April: Chemo Day

Today is the day I receive the second part of the chemo – the final three poisons, which are different from the first three.

Mum
At 1pm we went to the hospital. They x-rayed the lump in Carolann's neck. It was 6pm before we got home. She had the usual reaction to the chemo taste, smell, itchy nose etc. She was exhausted. Poor little girl.

Today was another close call. As the nurse came to give me my chemo, she called me 'Carol'. Now normally, this annoys me as my name is Carolann. But today I just said, 'Yes' and she started setting up and preparing to administer the poison to me. Just as she was about to administer it, another nurse said, 'Wait! I think we have the chemo mixed up!'

It turned out there was another patient on the ward, also called Carol, her middle name was Ann, and her surname was pronounced the same as mine. How much of a coincidence was that? Phew! That was a close call! When they checked my date of birth, they realised it was indeed wrong. Can you imagine if they had given me her cocktail? Along with the cocktail still in my system, I may have grown another bloody head!

Tuesday 3rd April: Day 1
Mum

A nurse came to the house today to give Carolann an injection of steroids in her stomach. Her stomach is so swollen up and they call this chemo belly. Carolann stayed in bed as her bones were aching and she felt tired and sick. The weather was miserable today, just like our lives at present. It was snowy, windy and very cold. Carolann was having such a bad time. She couldn't speak due to her sore throat. Jenna had to take her to the hospital for a blood test. They said she had an infection and gave her antibiotics. She was very ill again. Please God, Our Lady, Saint Ann please please help her.

Friday 6th April: Day 4

Carolann was still very ill, she had a high temperature, a sore throat, thrush in her mouth, her bones ached and she was suffering from sickness, a headache and vomiting. I wished they would take her into hospital and care for her properly. All this and the chemo is really affecting her poor little body. She rang the hospital and they were concerned about her. I think they want to admit her.

Sunday 8th April: Day 6

Carolann's temperature was now 38.1. They admitted her into the cancer hospital. She had what looked like shingles on her boob – I was so worried. She was on an antibiotic drip for twenty-four hours. She had a full-blown infection and was very poorly. As well as her temperature, she had diarrhoea, thrush on her tongue and her mouth was still full of sores. She didn't like the ward she was on, but I was relieved to know they were monitoring her. They couldn't get her temperature down, which was a worry. She couldn't stand the smell of the cleaning chemicals.

Tuesday 10th April: Day 8

She couldn't sleep last night because of the drip; it was hurting her vein. She was distressed and wanted to go home, poor sick girl. She has a problem with her teeth as well. But she does seem a little bit better. The antibiotics must have started to work at last. My precious girl, these are sad days. They took the cannula out and put her on oral antibiotics. She was still very ill but wanted to go home. Carolann had been very frustrated with the nursing staff and didn't want any further antibiotics in her vein. They didn't understand that she was really suffering with the taste of any liquid going into her veins. She was so sensitive to smells and didn't want any more treatment. The staff didn't understand how badly she was suffering. This was the first time I had ever heard Carolann swear. Another Doctor came to speak to her and he was very nice with her. He took more blood from her and they were going to try and identify the infection. She had calmed down a bit. By the way, it was only one swear word and I've heard a lot worse!

Thursday 12th April: Day 10

During the night she had a fever of 38.8. Her sheets were soaking.

She phoned me at 06.30am to say that she felt better. I was not convinced. If she can get her temperature below 38C they will let her go home. Jenna was suffering watching her mum. She acts indifferent, but I knew she was in pain.

Friday 13th April: Day 11
At last, at 2pm, they let her come home with antibiotics. They said the infection had been caused by the side effects of the chemo. At least we had her home and could look after her again.

A Broken Thermometer

So, I ended up in the cancer hospital as I had a temperature, sore throat, ulcers and a sore mouth and I felt just awful. I didn't want to go into hospital, but I think even I knew how poorly I was becoming and I couldn't risk my life. I could no longer look after myself and I needed to get on top of the infection. I was put in a side room for assessment before being transferred to the ward. They started me on antibiotics straight away. I told the nurse I was no good with smells or tastes, which I don't think she quite understood, and when she put the cannula in my arm and flushed it through, I immediately tasted the flush, even though it was only water and I told her I was going to be sick. She just left the room and didn't come back, so Jed had to find me a sick bowl because I vomited violently. The nurse didn't return to help or check on me. Great nursing skills!

Why have nursing staff working on a cancer ward if they're not aware or sympathetic to all the symptoms patients go through? And where was her empathy? Basic nursing skills include fetching a vomiting patient a sick bowl, helping them freshen up, or even just checking they're okay. That would have been nice.

I was curled up in the bed and knew I'd made the right decision to come to hospital, even though I didn't want to be there. I was eventually moved up to a ward then given a side room as I had a little rash under my arm and some diarrhoea (nothing bad but I knew I would get a side ward if they thought I had diarrhoea) to make sure I was separate from the other cancer patients.

I was told to stay in my room at all times. It was so clean I struggled with all the smells – it smelt like antiseptic or alcohol and I had to tell them they couldn't clean my room whilst I was in it. I even had to remove the antiseptic handwash as I couldn't bear to look at the word 'alcohol'. I could imagine the smell and the taste and it made me feel sick. My sense of smell was so sensitive. I didn't think the nursing staff understood just how bad it was and this made me angry. (No wonder I swore in front of my mum!) I'm sure they thought I was being over-dramatic. The cleaning staff had to mop my floor with just hot water and no chemicals, and their faces told me, they were not impressed!

You know, I never touched a drop of alcohol for nearly two years after this as the mere thought of the word and the smell associated with it made me gag! And once, when I walked through a shopping centre, a lady sprayed perfume for me to smell and I gagged. The smell was revolting to my senses!

The nurses kept taking my temperature but it remained high. I had no idea why it was still elevated after a couple of days on antibiotics; I was actually feeling a lot better after a few days of treatment. They kept taking blood samples to send to the lab to see what was happening with my white blood cells, in a bid to find out what infection was causing the high temperature. Eventually, I got to the stage where I refused to have any more blood taken. The nursing staff were coming into my room throughout the day and night to take blood. How much blood did they need? My arm and vein were becoming sore. I don't think the nurse was very happy that I refused the procedure and she told me that she would have to report it to the nurse in charge that night: the matron. I think it was at that point that I swore and nearly gave my poor mum a heart attack! Did they think that by threatening me with the matron I'd be scared and change my mind? I am not a bloody child! If I don't want any more blood taken, it's my right to refuse them. So, go on nursey, snitch on me to matron – I really don't care and I told her so!

The matron arrived that night and she was actually very nice. I told her I didn't want any more blood taken as my arm was beginning to hurt due to the amount already taken. She asked me to let her do it one last time and assured me she would be very gentle. I think I was at the end of my tether and she could see that. I let her take my blood as she sat and spent some time with me, listened to what was bothering me, and seemed to understand. If she'd been as offish as the others, I would not have given in. It was nice to have someone actually listen to my concerns and understand how I was feeling. This is how to nurse.

I had not mixed with any other cancer patients so

being in a cancer hospital was the first time I realised just how many others there were like me. All of us fighting the same fight but with our own personal battles. I stood by my door looking around the ward and saw lots of male patients with large burns and holes in their necks partially covered up by bandages. It resembled something from a war film and I was shocked by what some of these patients had been through and were enduring. Those poor men! Yes, *men*; I later discovered I'd been put on a male ward for throat cancer as there was no other side rooms available. This must have been the reason why the nursing staff didn't know how to care for me properly and had been asking me daft questions. As one nurse confirmed, they 'weren't used to working with breast cancer patients.' This was why they were confused by some of the things I'd said to them.

To this day I still do not understand that claim; I was in a cancer hospital with an infection caused by chemo. It was nothing to do my breast cancer, so surely, they knew how to treat a patient with an infection? And the doctors must have had knowledge on the subject; they must work in different areas of the hospital. None of it made any sense. I just needed treatment for my infection, and care and compassion, in short, basic nursing care. The only person who showed me any empathy was the night matron, so thank you, nurse, for threatening me with her, and thank you, matron, for being so kind.

Being a nurse myself I have learnt so much about treating patients. I'd always known I was a great nurse and loved looking after my patients, but now I knew I would give them even more care and compassion. When you are poorly and frightened and need a friendly, caring face –

someone to look after you when you are so low – you would expect that from nurses. So, to the nurse who didn't get me a vomit bowl when I told her I was about to be sick; to the nurses who rolled their eyes because I couldn't stand the smell of the cleaning solution; to the nurses who pulled faces when I was at the end of my tether and didn't want any more blood tests, shame on you. You wear your uniform with pride and should treat your patients with respect and dignity. I wasn't trying to be annoying – I was ill and needed care and empathy. When I had been told I was being admitted into hospital, I was relieved – I knew I needed care because I was so unwell – I just wanted to go into hospital and be looked after. I was asking too much apparently!

On my last night in hospital a newly qualified nurse came to do my temperature and, again, it was high. I told her this couldn't be right; I felt well. She told me I would need more bloods taken but I stopped her straight away: 'No, that's not going to happen'.

I told her to take my temperature again. She did and it was still up. Something wasn't right. I asked her to take her own temperature. She looked surprised but I insisted. She did and ha! It was as high as mine. I said, 'You need to get into this bed and have bloods taken!'

I knew something was wrong. It turned out the thermometer was broken and was not giving a true reading. This was confirmed when she found another thermometer and it proved my temperature was back to normal. I knew I felt better! All those needless blood tests, trying to work out what was going on and it was just a faulty thermometer! This was just one more thing that was wrong with the nursing care I received during this journey. I had been using the same thermometer the whole time I was in there to stop the spread of infection, so God knows how long it had been reading incorrectly. At least we got to the bottom of the problem in the end. And, crucially, it meant I could go home. Yeyyy!

Thursday 19th April: Day 17
Mum
Carolann got a letter from her ex-husband's lawyer today. She was so unhappy and ill, and now this letter. Can things get any worse?

Friday 20th April: Day 18
Carolann had to go to hospital for a blood test. Then we went to see her lawyer. I hate her ex doing this to her. She is so depressed and ill with the chemo. She does not need this added stress.

They are an ex for a reason

A few days ago, I received a letter from my ex-husband's solicitor. And by ex, I mean ex, whom I divorced a few years earlier having been separated from him for even longer. I won't even give him a false name – he doesn't deserve that – and by giving him a name, any name, might suggest I remotely cared. The truth is I have absolutely no feelings for this man, good or bad. He is not on any of my radars and, as much as he tried to hurt me when I was at my lowest point, I still have no hatred or bad feelings towards him. That would just bring bad karma. He just doesn't register in my life. His timing of trying to gain money out of me wasn't great, but he knew exactly what he was doing. If only he had come to me saying he needed money, he would have found himself in a better position than he did at the end of the court case! I would always have helped him – he just didn't realise that at the time. What a shame! Anyway, it appeared he wanted a fight and he seriously underestimated how good I was at fighting. Did he not remember living with me? If I could fight this battle each month and survive, I could fight him, and fight I would!

I was so poorly and weak and yet I had to attend court on many occasions, which seemed very unfair. I needed to be at home resting and trying to get well not sitting in a court room. The judge even once said to me, 'Just because you have cancer doesn't mean we can show you sympathy. We need to treat you both the same.'

How bad was that? The judge came across as a male chauvinist and from day one he made it clear he didn't like me, or women in general.

One day, when we were in court, I forgot myself and started clapping at something that had been said. The judge and solicitors were not happy but I was past caring. The judge looked at me with disgust. I actually wished he would bang his gavel and shout, 'Silence in court!' It would have made a great story, but instead he just glared at me. He was such a horrible man and plainly didn't like women. So, there I was, stuck in a court room when I should have been at home recovering. It was so unfair that I wasn't allowed to concentrate fully on my illness and recovery. Instead, all my energy was being used on the court case.

Ultimately, it didn't end as well as he hoped. At the last minute I managed to get a really good barrister who sorted a fair deal out for us both. My solicitor up until that point hadn't been great; he resembled Columbo with his long grey coat, scruffy appearance, and a plastic bag, in which he carried all his paperwork. His office resembled something from the 1980s. The magazines he had were as dated as the wallpaper (1970s woodchip). Even in court he was told off by the judge for shuffling papers and rooting about in his plastic bag. It was like being at the cinema when people open sweets and make a noise – he was constantly rummaging around looking for something. At one point the judge shouted, 'Will you put that bag down and be quiet! Stop messing about with your papers!'

How embarrassing! But I didn't blame the judge; I also wanted to shout at him to stop bloody rooting and listen to what's being said! Jesus, it was like having a child representing me!

So, he was an ex for many reasons, but his behaviour when I was very poorly was unforgivable. I remained the bigger person and after the hearing ended, I shook his hand and said, 'No more now – I don't want to fight with you anymore.'

My barrister said, 'That was a very noble thing to do.'

And that was that chapter of my life over with. Now to concentrate on this battle!

Monday 23rd April: Chemo Day
Mum

Today is the second session of the second part of chemo. We're nearly at the final one. Thank God. At 1pm Carolann had her chemo. Today we bought ice lollies and she was sucking on them. We bought a box of eight and she had six. They were melting due to the heat. We wanted the nurses to hurry up and get the chemo started before they all melted. It was their idea to bring ice lollies to stop her having to taste the chemo. She took the chemo better with the ice lollies – it blocked the nasty taste.

I See the Finishing Line

Because I was struggling with the taste of the chemo, the nurse suggested I bring ice lollies in to suck whilst they administered it. The ice lollies were melting due to the heat, (it was a very hot day) but it worked a little. I had got to a stage where I was struggling even to get to hospital to have my treatment. I felt like I was having a panic attack the minute I arrived there. My body didn't want it anymore and was doing everything in its power to prevent me from going in. I was experiencing fight or flight symptoms again and my mind was urging me to take the latter. But I couldn't. I had to try and overcome this.

They offered to give me some drugs so I was more relaxed, which may have made it easier for me to go in, but I didn't fancy taking any more tablets. I was already on such a cocktail of medication. But it was getting harder and harder just walking into the hospital as I knew what was to come. My body was saying no more and sending me into melt down. I just wanted to cry.

I had to sit and talk to the nurses before I could go onto the ward. I was tearful and stressed out. The treatment was so harsh on my body from the second it entered my vein. Chemotherapy takes a lot out of you; you feel like you are taken to the brink of death, then just as you're about to die, they bring you back and a few days later it starts all over again. It was exhausting and I felt like I was being tortured. It would have been easier if they could have put me to sleep for six months whilst they administered the chemo, then when I woke up it would have all been over.

Wednesday 25th April: Day 2
Mum

Carolann has 'chemo brain' and is forgetting things, so a court hearing at this time was not great for her. She started with a sore throat again, her bones are aching and she is exhausted. It's so hard to get her to take fluids, she has such a horrible taste in her mouth — she says it tastes of chemicals. She texted me this morning and said she fancies porridge. She was in bed with a lot of pain. She was so tired and hardly touched her porridge. She didn't want the blinds open; her face was yellow and her eyes were red. She looked so ill. My lovely Carolann. What can I do?

Friday 27th April: Day 4

Carolann had suffered a terrible night. She had a temperature, sweating and nightmares. She can't eat though she fancies juicy plums, so I went to get her some. This was another easy one to fulfil. Her bones ache and her tongue is covered in sores. She is trying to sip water, but her tooth is sore. She was in bed ill all day. She had nightmares again last night, which will be from the chemo.

Monday 7th May: Day 14

She is having trouble with her tooth but is unable to go to the dentist due to the risk of infection whilst she has chemo. She tried to make an appointment but the dentist said no. The chemo is affecting her gums and teeth. She's using mouth wash and is really looking after her mouth and teeth. She has a broken tooth and is worried about the colour of her teeth, as they're usually so white, it's such a shame. She also looks very pale today. She has pain in her legs, and is shaking, but otherwise not a bad day.

Saturday 12th May: Day 19

Carolann has seen small brown hairs on her scalp and is so pleased. Her hair is finally starting to grow back!

Monday 14th May 2012: Last Chemo Day – Yay Hey!

This should be the last of six sessions of chemotherapy. We went to the hospital for 1pm as usual. Ryan came with us. We spoke to two other female patients. One of whose cancer had spread and this made Carolann worry. Ryan took lots of photos of his mum receiving the chemo, even one of the empty drip bag, so funny! Carolann sucked on her ice lollies again. She was so worn out when we got home at 5pm. I was also really tired, just with the stress of it all.

Tuesday 15th May: Day 1

She has slept well; the nurse came and gave her the injection of steroids into her stomach again. This steroid injection helps protect her vital organs from the chemo. This is the LAST steroid

injection she will get. Carolann spoke with the nurse for over an
hour. I am glad she did this – she needed to get a lot of things off
her mind.

The nurse told me that when this was all over, I might have a day when I just break down and cry. I thought she was mad! Why would I do that? I had nearly finished the treatment so why would I go backwards and start crying? I had a good chat with her though, as I had a lot going on in my head and needed to speak to someone outside of the family as I didn't want to upset them. She advised me to go to a place where I could receive support and where they had counsellors who could help me come to terms with what I'd been through. I don't want to go to a place like that and discuss things with strangers. No, that's not for me. (Watch this space: how wrong I was!)

Friday 18th May: Day 4
Mum
Carolann was suffering again and she had a very bad night. She had aching bones, was sweating, she was yellow and looked very ill. She had red eyes and a sore tongue. She can't eat or drink again. She cried when Jed got home. He is so good with her. But this is unusual for Carolann – she doesn't really cry, especially in front of us.

Sunday 20th May 2012: Day 6
Another bad day. She had a fever, pains in her stomach, aching bones, tiredness, and sickness. Poor, poor Carolann. This is HELL. She cannot enjoy any food. It is so awful having to watch your child suffer like this. As her mum I want to take away her pain but

I can't. There is nothing I can do to make this any easier for her. She fancies Ricicles. This is a new request for us. She's keeping us on our toes! I went to every supermarket looking for them but I couldn't find them anywhere. All the family took this task on but this time she had us. Do they even make them any more?

Sunday 27th May: Day 13

Today I went to watch The Race for Life. One of my students was running the race for me, which was a lovely gesture. We arrived at the park and I had to walk to a particular area where we were going to sit and watch her run past. It took me ages to walk to the spot. I was so tired and out of breath and I was really struggling to walk. When she ran past, she was wearing a T-shirt with my name and face on, and when she saw me, she ran up to me and gave me a pink rose. I thought this was a really nice touch and so caring of her. I have never had my face on a T-Shirt before, and being a face within the crowd of runners was a very poignant moment for me. It was also very emotional watching the runners with messages to those people they had loved and lost to cancer on their T-Shirts. I was so lucky and blessed to be a survivor.

Strong Beautiful Inspirational Women.

Monday 28th May: Day 14

So today I went to a charity cancer care facility. I know I had said I wouldn't go, but curiosity got the better of me and I thought I would go along, just the once, and see what it was all about.

When I arrived, a very nice lady took me into a sitting room, where lots of other people sat around talking to each other. I appeared to be the youngest in the room and sat alone on a sofa. I was completely out of my comfort zone. This was a twelve-week programme with a morning and afternoon session. I had told them I would not be staying for the afternoon session, which was 'Relaxation'. I do not like things like this; I can't relax at the best of times and would have felt very awkward trying to relax with other people. I'm one of those people who would close their eyes, then have one eye open watching everyone else, then I would laugh and spoil it all for the others. So, no it was definitely not for me. I would stay for the morning – a counselling session then a treatment, (you got a massage or treatment of your choice), have my lunch then go home.

As I sat there, I heard a lady talking. She was telling another lady that she had just found out that her cancer had spread and she was now terminal. And then it happened. Remember me telling you the nurse had said it would hit me and I would break down? Well she was right! It was like a switch had been flicked and all of a sudden, I realised what I had been through, and that, even though I was coming out the other side, cancer could still come back for me, claiming my life like it had with so many others.

I sat there with tears rolling down my face and I could not stop them. Everyone was looking at me but for the first time ever I didn't care. It was like a dam had burst inside me. Tears and snot ran down my face. One of the staff members asked if I wanted to come with her and I nodded and followed her like a lost puppy. She took me into a room to meet my counsellor who offered me a tiny little tissue. Never mind a tissue, I needed a towel! I sat with the counsellor and just sobbed my heart out, the biggest fattest tears ever. She said nothing; she just let me cry until I had cried enough.

I think I must have cried for about an hour, until my time was up in fact, which was a shame. Everyone had been encouraging me to cry, but up to this point I'd been reluctant to show my emotions. Then, just when I had got into the swing of it, showing every emotion I had, they put a time limit on it. If a stage actor had delivered a performance like the one I'd just given, they'd have been presented with an Olivier award! But how do you then bring yourself down after being so emotional? This was something else I had to learn to do and I found myself glancing at the clock, knowing that I could only cry for so long because when my time was nearly up, I had to start pulling myself together again. Now I had to learn how to cry for just fifty-five minutes, then switch off! All these skills I had to learn weren't easy!

The counsellor once tried to do a relaxation technique with me, but it was so uncomfortable sitting in a small room with someone who was telling you to close your eyes and relax. I kept opening my eyes to see what she was actually doing. It felt so awkward and, suffice to say, this technique didn't work for me.

Over the weeks I told my counsellor everything, including my fears and worries about the future and for the first few sessions I literally just cried while she sat and watched me (which was uncomfortable, I must admit). I poured my heart out to her, sharing my most intimate secrets. I told her all about my journey – all the ups and downs ¬– but as some of the story was amusing, the counsellor seemed to be getting more out of the sessions than me! She would love to hear my stories each week and would have a right giggle, apologising for laughing: 'I'm so sorry Carolann but it is just so funny!'

Eventually my tears dried up, which was good, so we just talked about everyday life. Sometimes she told me her worries and fears and, on these days,, I wanted to swap chairs with her; our roles were changing. We talked until, eventually, I had nothing more to say and I think I'd helped her through most of her troubles too, so the counselling came to a natural end. The sessions were becoming awkward as counsellors are not supposed to ask you questions. So, to try and avoid these awkward silences, I felt I had to prepare discussion points each week. This is when you know it's time for the sessions to end. My counsellor thanked me and said I had been a great support to her, and she'd thoroughly enjoyed our sessions. A little bit back to front perhaps.

For anyone thinking about counselling after any trauma, illness, or anything else that may be worrying you, I can definitely recommend it. Give it a try, even just one session. You never know, it may help you … or your counsellor!

Whilst at this facility I met a lovely lady whom I will call Dina. She'd had breast cancer 11 years previously and it had returned, which worried me. So many people get it back again many years later. Dina and I would laugh together, acting like teenagers back at school – we had so much fun. Sometimes the facility was a very quiet place and all you could hear was Dina and me giggling in the corridors, which brought the place alive. We even went on a course together at the facility, but there was only the two of us there, which was terrible for the tutor. We couldn't stop laughing and messing about. The two of us really hit it off and had so much fun. And although we were acting like kids again, it was what we both needed after the year we'd both endured. The facility had become my little hidden treasure – my escape from all the madness – and now I had a good friend there as well, which made my weekly visits so much more fun.

I would do my usual trick of running ahead of Dina and hiding. I would jump out and scare her shitless. It never impressed her but always made me laugh. I was always careful after the consultant episodes that it was actually Dina I was jumping out at and not someone else. Some of the people in the facility were quite frail and the last thing they needed was me scaring them silly!

They provided lovely lunches at the centre for just £2.50. For this price you got dinner, dessert, and a drink. They even served alcohol, which seemed strange to me, but we indulged anyway just to be polite. I began to really enjoy these days with my new buddy, and soon we were meeting up for coffee and lunch. One day, after the course had come to an end, Dina and I met at a garden centre and she confided in me that she was suffering with pain in her hip, which was a worry. I urged her to ask for pain relief from her consultant, but she was worried if she took it now, she wouldn't benefit from it later on when the pain became worse.

I was worried about my friend and the next time we were due to meet for lunch, she cancelled as her pain had become worse. The cancer had returned. I was devastated for her. The pain took hold of her so quickly that I never got to see her again. I never had the chance to say goodbye and just two months later her daughter phoned to let me know she had passed away. I remember my response was, 'You're joking?' which was a strange and stupid thing to say, as if she would joke about her mother passing away. I was devastated.

I went to Dina's funeral alone as I wanted to be able to cry without upsetting Jed or anyone else. I drove to the church and I was already crying in the car. I remember the hearse was parked up with Dina's casket inside, and I had to overtake it to drive into the car park. Trust Dina to be early for her funeral!

This was a dreadful experience. The weather was beautiful and there were a lot of people at the funeral, but I knew no one. I sat on a bench in the sun and cried, I couldn't stop myself. I was an emotional wreck. The tears were big fat ones and I had the smallest piece of tissue, which was falling apart. My nose was running, my eyes were streaming and there was nothing I could do to stop. I was sobbing so loudly, and getting louder, (something new to me) and people started to notice (probably wondering who the hell I was). I was the only one outside the church sobbing. And sobbing looks so much uglier than crying, but that was me: tears and snot and wailing like a banshee. (Did you know a banshee is a fairy-woman who appears at the site of an imminent death in the middle of the night and lets out a chilling high-pitched wailing sound?)

A woman came over and asked if I was OK. It was Dina's best friend. Now I'm sure this wasn't a coincidence – out of the hundreds of people at the funeral, any one of them could have approached me but I know Dina had sent her best friend to console me. The people at the funeral had been watching me as I was a wreck, and no one knew who I was. My make-up was non-existent with my drawn-on eyebrows now wiped away (these had not regrown following my hair loss). I was not a pretty sight but I didn't care. I was past the point of no return. It was as if a river had burst its banks and nothing was going to stop the flow. I had to empty myself of tears if that was even possible.

I once read that when someone dies, their spirit can sometimes wait around to watch their funeral. The book claimed that a week in human life was the equivalent to a day in the afterlife. Now, I don't know if this is true, but I am sure Dina was at her funeral watching us all and had seen me upset. Dina and I once had a conversation about this, and we had both said we would stay and watch our own funeral to be nosy and see who turned up. So, I'm adamant that Dina was watching over us and that's why, out of all the people there, she chose her best friend to console me. It was a sign from her to me. If anyone else had approached me, I would think differently; that it was just someone being nice. But Dina's best friend said she'd been watching me and had a sudden urge to speak to me. This was Dina's doing!

Whilst at the facility we had many conversations with other cancer sufferers and survivors, and we all agreed that a funeral was a great way of healing and getting rid of all the emotions we'd been carrying around with us. There was nowhere else you could have a good cry without upsetting a family member and, sometimes, you just needed to cry until you could cry no more – it really did help with the healing process. We all understood each other because we were all on the same path and had all suffered the same stress.

Dina's friend said, 'Come on,' and took my hand, leading me past the big queue of people waiting to get into the church. We walked past her family and friends up to the front of the queue. I heard people whispering and the whispers worked their way up the queue as we walked past:

'Who's that?'

'That's her cancer buddy.'

Dina must have told them that as this wasn't a phrase I'd heard before, but it gave me comfort. We walked into the church but I decided I could not go any further. I didn't want to watch her funeral. I was too emotional. I tried to turn back but there were so many people around me I couldn't move. I was trapped, being pushed forward by the throng of people. The next thing I knew I was seated in a pew a few rows from the front with Dina's family. I couldn't see anything as I was too small to see over everyone and it was standing room only. It was so busy; Dina had so many friends and family. Although the church was packed, it was so quiet you could hear a pin drop. The only sound was the vicar saying his sermon, but as the service went ahead all you could hear over vicar's soft voice was me sobbing loudly for both Dina and myself. At that moment, the whole journey was too much for me. It was so unfair for Dina and anyone else who became the victim of this nasty disease.

At the end of the service I passed a card to her daughter. The card was full of things that Dina had told me about her daughter and her new grandchild, and there were lots of

249

funny stories that I thought her daughter might like. For example, Dina had been really amused when her daughter was preparing her overnight bag to go into hospital to have her baby and she had packed hair straighteners. This tickled Dina and she'd said, 'She has no idea! She thinks she'll have time to straighten her hair!'

Lots of little things had tickled her and I wrote a lot of them down – all things Dina had shared with me.

Her best friend invited me to the pub to have a drink afterwards but I declined. I couldn't cope anymore and I left the church and headed back to the bench to get myself together before I drove home. It was such a beautiful bright warm day and I felt at peace sitting on the bench in the quiet of the crematorium. I felt at ease in this environment, and it gave me some comfort. The day looked perfect with the sun shining in a blue cloudless sky. I could just hear the faint sounds of the birds singing in the nearby trees. I was struck by the contrast of such a beautiful day being filled with so much sadness at my friend's passing.

Everyone left the church to go to the pub and I was alone on my bench. I was exhausted by the time I got home and fervently hoped I would never have to attend another funeral.

I have done my best to support the cancer facility over the years, raising small amounts of money through the dance school. I have attended their charity balls, bringing over a hundred of my friends and mums from the dance school, and I have provided dancers for their charity lunches. Once again, I was taken out of my comfort zone when I was asked to be a survivor model for their charity ladies' lunch. This was terrifying, but I overcame my fears and managed to walk down the catwalk with pride for all those women who had lost their lives to breast cancer, and for all those who had survived.

I was also featured on one of their promotional videos. Every little helps, as they say and I wanted to ensure this wonderful place remained opened so that other people needing their support could access it. I wanted to give something back for all the support they had given me and Dina and, as I was to discover, another lovely lady and her family, that I was soon to be introduced to.

If I thought I had been taken out of my comfort zones before, the next challenge would test all my nerves and bravery: I was asked to stand up and give a speech at their charity ball about my journey. This was a terrifying experience. As I waited to take the stand, I was so nervous and felt sick. I tried to breathe and keep calm but my heart was racing so fast. I hadn't even told my friends who had come to the ball with me; I wanted to keep it to myself as they would have made me even more nervous. Their faces were a picture as I stood up and took the stand. They had asked me to do a ten-minute speech, but I had so much to say I actually spoke for fifteen minutes! I had been practising for weeks.

The first line of my speech was, 'I am shitting myself!' which was not what I had written but it was how I felt at the time and it broke the ice. I conquered my fears and stood up in front of a room full of people, all of whom were listening to me, and I spoke from the heart. Every pair of eyes was on me and the silence in the room confirmed they were all listening to me.

After the speech many people complimented me and

said it was a really good speech. My family were at the ball that night and we had my mum on FaceTime as she was in Spain, so she could also hear and see my speech. I have to say I was very proud of myself for doing it and it was good to push myself to the limits of what I thought I could do. That said, I wouldn't like to do it again!

I knew most of the ladies who worked at the cancer support centre and had formed some wonderful relationships with some of them, especially a very special lady I will call 'Ava'. She became a dear friend and when she left the facility along with other ladies I knew, I was very sad. Not having that special contact – someone who had made it very personal to me – meant I eventually lost contact with the facility. It was the end of another era but I also felt that I'd moved on; I was stronger now and no longer needed this level of support. That special touch that Ava gave to everyone who supported the facility ensured that they, in return, continued to support it; she made everyone feel so special. I am still in touch with her today and I now support the new charity she works with.

Ava had introduced me to another lovely lady who was using the facility. This happened just as the dance school was lucky enough to get involved in Take That's Manchester tour. We were part of the voluntary cast and got to support the group on stage at Manchester Arena. I provided more than twenty people for the event and decided to let someone at the facility who really loved Take That take part in this once-in-a-lifetime event. Ava told me this lady was a massive Take That fan and had been to all their concerts apart from this last one. Her husband hadn't booked it due to her illness. So, when

Ava told her what I had offered she was over the moon.

The day I met Kirsty she said she thought it was a wind-up and could not believe it. She was half expecting someone to jump out with a camera and say, 'Got you!'

We hit it off straight away and shared lots of similarities with the treatment and the symptoms we had both endured. We both had 'chemo brain' which was hilarious because the two of us would stutter and forget words, meaning every conversation was a challenge as well as a laugh. Kirsty was only 33 when she died and her story was heart-breaking. I will try and share it. This is what she told me:

Kirsty had first been diagnosed with breast cancer at the age of 27 years old. She had a lumpectomy as part of her treatment. She then found a second lump not long after. As she had had two diagnoses so close together, they did the blood test to see if she was carrying the BRCA gene. The blood test revealed she was carrying the faulty gene so she had a double mastectomy. She was then told to go away and enjoy her life which she did. Kirsty did not need to be told to enjoy her life, she already loved life, and this was enriched even more when she married Scott, the father of her son who was seven years old when I met her. Following her wedding both Kirsty and Scott enjoyed some worry free time, before she unfortunately found a third lump around February time. This lump, however, was misdiagnosed as 'scar tissue' by her consultant! All he did was feel the lump with his fingers. No scan and no biopsy was offered. He was not worried and he told her to stop worrying and just to enjoy her life. Kirsty fell pregnant again and the lump continued to grow. By around August they went back to see the consultant as they were concerned about its size.

This lump was diagnosed as cancerous and Kirsty was sadly given her terminal diagnosis. She had twelve to eighteen months to live. The worst news any person could receive, and more so for Kirsty because the consultant had got it wrong in the first place. She was advised to terminate her pregnancy which was one of the hardest things she had ever had to do. Kirsty now had to face even more really tough decisions regarding her treatment, as if she hadn't gone through enough already. Not many people know about the pregnancy, but her husband Scott wanted to highlight this as this shows all the crappy stuff a cancer diagnosis can involve and more importantly it shows what a ridiculous amazing strong woman Kirsty was. A cancer diagnosis can turn a person's whole world up-side-down. Why do these consultants still get it wrong? All he had to do was scan her or give her a biopsy. Like my original misdiagnosis, this happens all the time and people are losing their lives because they trust the consultant's word. If only they had scanned her scar tissue, they would have realised this was a new cancer. I cannot say if she would have survived but it would be helpful if consultants stopped second-guessing lumps and had them all checked out, regardless of their assumptions.

They got Kirsty's diagnosis wrong and she paid the price for it. This is so unfair and so wrong. And I say again, listen to your gut feeling, you know your own body better than anyone else and if you are not happy, seek a second opinion. Doctors are just human beings like you and me; they sometimes make mistakes and get things wrong. Always push for that extra test and never put all your trust into the hands of doctors.

Kirsty was such a beautiful positive person. Even with her terminal diagnosis, Scott said she remained a strong and amazing women and still managed to find so much fun and laughter, allowing her to have the most amazing times and build lasting memories in her last two years, which is a massive testament to her. We had so many good times with her in her final year. We attended the charity balls, drank lots of alcohol and danced and had the best of times. She would come and visit me and we would have very frank discussions. She told me all the plans she had made for her funeral. She said one of the mums at the school gate had said how brave she was and she didn't like that comment. She said she wasn't brave, she was terrified. She said bravery is when you choose to confront something that frightens you and takes you out of your comfort zone. Although she was facing her fear head on, this wasn't something she had chosen to do – she had no choice. And she was scared, she told me so. As a friend I wanted so much to help her but all I could do was listen, and because I had been through cancer, I could have frank and open discussions with her. We only had a few of these conversations – the rest of the time she was her happy, funny self and we enjoyed our time together.

So, Kirsty came to the dance school to learn the routines for the Take That event. I also invited her two sisters so they could all enjoy the experience together. It was so much fun and very exciting. She loved doing the Take That concert and when Mark Owen sat on her knee, she nearly had a heart attack! As part of the act, we were pretending to play a violin and she was so involved in what she was doing, she didn't see Mark approach her.

I was trying to get her attention, but it was so loud at the arena and she was wearing a radio mic, so he sat on her knee before she knew it. Her face was a picture. We had planned for her to sit in the special chair – the one Mark always went to (he would sit on the knee of whoever was there). Anyway, Kirsty remained professional and carried on playing her 'violin'. I remember looking over at her as we were plunged into darkness and Take That sang *Rule the World*. Over 10,000 people had their camera torches on, lighting up the arena. I struggled not to get emotional as I saw her face and wondered what she was thinking as she watched all the lights in the arena.

One of the hardest things she had to do was to prepare her young son for her death. She told me that as his mum, it was her job to keep him safe and happy, and yet she was going to be the person responsible for breaking his little heart and turning his whole world upside down. This was such a sad thing for her to say. She made many visits to the facility, where they helped her to come to terms with her diagnosis and helped her prepare to hand her son over to the counsellors. One day we both sat at the facility and she looked up at the counsellor and said, 'It's time for you to have my son. Please look after him.'

This one line made my heart burst. This was so sad and, once again, so unfair. She knew her time was coming to an end. Some of the things she told me broke my heart.

After more than a year of fighting her battle, Kirsty passed away. She had kept in touch for the last few weeks by text messages and told me her stomach was swelling up and no matter how many times they drained it, it filled up again. She was in so much pain and said she felt like she was on fire inside and as they put one fire out another one would start in a different place in her body.

She sent me a final message which was the worst but most beautiful message I have ever received. It said this:

Thank you for being my friend, and thank you for everything you have done for me, but I am getting near to the end of my life and the pain is all too much for me so I am going into the hospice.

I tried to text her back but she never responded. I am sure she would have been told to do it this way. You say goodbye to everyone and then you leave it at that. No back and forward with the conversation. I understand this has to be the way but I was so so sad. It must have been the hardest journey in the world for her, knowing she was leaving her own house for the last time, and when she walked into the hospice, knowing she would never leave. This still breaks my heart.

It was a Saturday afternoon when she took a turn for the worse. Her sister kept messaging me. I was at dancing. Her sister joked, saying she was still here, hanging on. She had sent her husband and her little boy to football to keep the day as normal as possible for him. Kirsty was such a beautiful, thoughtful person right to the end. She passed away peacefully on the Saturday afternoon surrounded by her family.

This loss was even worse for me than Dina's and when I received the call at work, I was heartbroken. On the way home we popped into Asda and the song they had playing was *Rule the World* by Take That. The same song that had been playing at the concert; the same one when she watched all the lights shining in the arena, thousands of them, all lighting up the sky for her. I can't listen to this song without thinking about Kirsty.

Her funeral was arranged for a month later but I missed it as I was in Spain visiting my mum. Ava said it was just as well I wasn't there, as it was once of the saddest funerals she had ever attended and she knew how vulnerable I was. I thought about Kirsty all day on the day of her funeral. I may not have been there in person, but I was certainly there in spirit. Sleep well my dear friend. xx

When the time came to cut ties with the facility, it was a relief in one way as I didn't want to make any more friends I was going to lose; it was all just too sad. It was my time to live now. I am one of the lucky ones who had survived and if Dina or Kirsty could have been in my shoes, they would have ensured every day was lived to the max. I thank the facility for allowing me to meet these two, strong, inspirational, beautiful woman, but I could not take any more sadness; it was time for me to move on. I think about them all the time, and their families. And one thing I can do for these two inspirational women is to ensure I continue to raise awareness of breast cancer and continue raising money for the cancer support centre. They would have wanted other families in their situation to have the help and support they received so I will do my best in their memory starting with making a donation from every book sale I have. Never again will I take life for granted.

Good Riddance Chemo

Monday 4th June

Mum

This would have been chemo day – so glad it's not for Carolann and all the family. GOOD RIDDANCE CHEMO!

I gradually began to get better as the chemo disappeared from my system. I could feel myself getting stronger every day, though it took at least seven years before I was back to something that resembled the old me again. The tiredness was like a switch and remains so, even years later. It would get to 6pm and that was it: I couldn't do any more. One minute I would be OK, the next I would be exhausted. This is frustrating as it affects my life every day.

My consultant had told me about 'chemo brain' which was awful. The term is used to describe thinking and memory problems that cancer survivors can suffer from during and after cancer treatment. It's also known as 'chemo fog'. It causes cognitive impairment or cognitive dysfunction and can last for up to five years. I have forgotten so many things and I developed a stutter for a long time. This was to do with the effects the chemo (methotrexate) has on the white matter in the brain. Methotrexate causes a complex set of problems in three major cell types within the brain's white matter. My consultant told me to brain train but not to overdo it or put stress on the brain. I still have difficulty recalling names and events to this day, but it's nowhere near as bad as it was. The words are always on the tip of my tongue and can take me a few minutes to retrieve (this is where Google and Jed have helped!) It can be very frustrating and I'd be useless in a quiz team! My family play a game with me, trying to work out what word it is I'm trying to say. When I suddenly become stuck midway through a sentence and can't retrieve the next word, they all start shouting out different words. This goes on until either I remember what I want to say, or they guess the correct word for me! Sometimes they wait in anticipation to see what I am going to say, which can take a good few seconds before the word comes back to me and I can finish the sentence. At Christmas when it's time to play games, instead of charades or Monopoly, my adorable family shouts out, 'Let's play Guess what Nana is trying to say!'

At least I keep them amused!

As I had been warned, my prolapse, brought on by the chemo, became worse and I eventually had to have a hysterectomy. They tried various tricks to stop me from having to go through yet more surgery, one of which consisted of inserting a very thick non-pliable donut ring into my vagina. They claimed it was supposed to sit on the ridge that 'every woman has at the top of their vagina'. Not sure what that's all about … every time they pushed the ring into place and I stood up, it fell back down and protruded like a baby's head from my vagina! And believe me, each time they shoved it back up, the pain was excruciating. They told me I would have to see a gynaecologist and this was arranged for the following week.

I had not expected the next procedure: I was asked to strip off my bottom half and jump up on the bed. I lay in a room a bit like a theatre, which was strange, and there were nurses and a consultant all gowned up in their scrubs. They even had wellies on! Then they brought Jed into the room to hold my hand. What the hell were they about to do to me? I hadn't had a single conversation about what was to be done; I thought I was there to speak to the consultant about my prolapse and he would to examine me to see the extent of it. But before I knew it, I had my legs up in stirrups and the consultant was once again shoving what felt like an extra-large ring into my vagina.

It was obviously too large to insert but this consultant was not going to be beaten. As he shoved with all his strength, my bottom lifted off the bed and he actually moved me up the bed with his hand still inside my vagina. He looked like he was wearing a hand puppet! The pain felt like giving birth and I shouted, 'Fucking hell! What are you doing to me? STOP!'

He stopped what he was doing and said, 'This is not going to work.'

No shit Sherlock – I could have told you that as soon as you tried to shove an item inside me that was obviously too large to fit! I bet his mother never bought him plastic shape sorters – the ones where children learn to put the correct shape in the correct hole. The procedure felt like giving birth to a baby and then shoving the baby back up again headfirst. I was traumatised by it and because it had once again failed, they arranged for me to have surgery to fix the problem.

This also turned out to be an awful operation and I bled internally following surgery. Apparently, the blood sat in a pocket in my stomach instead of coming out through my vagina. They had told me to buy sanitary towels, which I did, and then I never had the need for them. I wonder if any of my procedures in the future will be straightforward.

One night the pain was so bad, I wanted to call an ambulance. But when I rang the nurse at the hospital for advice, she said, 'You've just had surgery – you will be sore'.

Not knowing what the pain was supposed to be like, and with the nurse assuming I was suffering with normal pain I just put up with it. I should have listened to my body. I knew something wasn't right. I had a great pain threshold, but this pain was excruciating. It was different to chemo pain but I knew it wasn't supposed to be this bad so I was worried.

The pain was no better after a couple of weeks and after I had pestered the life out of them to do something about it, they eventually scanned me and realised what had happened. Unfortunately, it was too late to do anything about it. The blood would dissolve naturally, just like the fluid in my back, so no treatment was necessary. I couldn't walk far because of the pain, which felt like a stitch but magnified by 1000, so once again I was struggling with my mobility.

During this time, we paid a visit to Ikea (which was a stupid thing to do when I was in so much pain, but that's me: I never learn) and halfway around the shop the pain became so excruciating it actually stopped me in my tracks. I was in the middle of Ikea and could not walk another step. I had to stand on the side of the trolley and be pushed the rest of the way by Jed. People were laughing, assuming I was just having fun and a little boy said to his mum, 'Can I go on the trolley like that lady, Mum?'

She replied quite firmly, 'No you can't. Don't be so silly – you're too old to be doing that!' What did I say about people judging you? If only she had known how much pain I was in and why I was hitching a ride on the trolley.

A Disastrous Trip to Spain

A couple of months after my last chemo I was able to go away, so we headed to my mum's house in Spain. On the way through airport security I was asked about my cap. They wanted me to remove it to make sure I wasn't concealing anything underneath it. There was no way I was removing this in the middle of a busy airport – *no way Jose*. I expected the inevitable (to be taken into a room, frisked and have my buttocks checked for drugs) and if that's what they had to do then so be it, but I was adamant: I was not removing my cap in public. To my disappointment, (it would have made a good story) they just patted it down. But it made me feel vulnerable and, once again, I attracted attention. Why did they have to make such a fuss? On the way back to England, Spanish security were much more compassionate; I just said 'cancer' and they were OK with that. They didn't even pat my head down.

It was in Spain where I took my cap off for the first time to reveal my hairless head in public — a massive achievement for me. It was so hot in the restaurants and I was struggling. Mum always asked if we could have a table away from people so I could have a bit more privacy and feel more comfortable when I removed my cap. That first time was scary but once it was off, it felt great to get the fresh air around my head. This must be how nudists feel on the beach. It is such a nice feeling to have air around your skin, especially on areas it doesn't normally get to. My head was sensitive to the warm air and it felt so refreshing and liberating. Who knows, I might have to try nude bathing! I've overcome so many fears throughout this journey and for that I'm proud of myself.

Back at the house Jed and I had just been to buy ice cream and I took some upstairs for my mum. On the way back down, my flip flops, which had no grip, slid on the step and there was nothing I could do. I flew up and landed hard on my coccyx on the marble staircase, then proceeded to hit every step as I fell down the entire marble staircase! I landed at the bottom in a heap and the pain that seared through my body was like no other pain I had ever felt. I couldn't move and knew I'd done some serious damage. My bottom was in a tight spasm and I felt sick and dizzy with the pain and shock of what had just happened. I had to get up off the floor. How I did it I do not know, but I used every ounce of strength I had and with the adrenaline rushing through my veins I managed to drag myself into the bedroom on the ground floor (which, luckily for me, was next to the stairs). I curled up on the bed in the foetal position and was unable to stretch my legs out. I was stuck in this position and the pain was searing through my body. Mum and Jed put ice packs on my bottom to try and ease some of the pain, but in the end, we had to phone an ambulance. The ice packs had melted, and my clothes were soaked through, but still I could not move.

I was desperate for the paramedics to arrive – I needed gas and air and pain relief. However, in Spain things are done a bit differently. So, when the ambulance arrived it didn't come with paramedics, just two men who work for the hospital doing transfers. There was no pain relief or gas and air. In short, they weren't equipped to deal with me. One of the men even had a sore wrist and had it strapped up! Between the two of them they had to put me in a transfer sheet and lift me onto a chair. I was still in the foetal position and unable to straighten my legs. The look on their faces when they tried to lift me was priceless. They didn't realise just how heavy I was and the man with the sore wrist nearly dropped me! It was at that point they realised I was wet through and must have thought I'd wet myself. Thank God my mum can speak Spanish and could tell them I was wet from the ice packs and nothing else!

They managed to get me into the ambulance but I was not very secure on the trolley. Mum came with me and Jed was to follow in the car. They told him which hospital I was going to and Jed knew roughly where it was so would get there no problem.

The ambulance drove off and I had to hold on for dear life as we went around corners at speed. I used my hands to push against whatever I could hold onto to stop myself from falling off the trolley. But then they decided to take me to a different hospital and the next thing we knew the sirens were on. Why did I suddenly need blue lights? Poor Jed, he couldn't keep up with the ambulance and was unaware we'd diverted to another hospital, so he was now heading to the wrong one.

On arrival at A&E I was left in a corridor as they were busy and had no beds. I didn't have my cap on and must have looked a sight with my half a dozen hairs that I'd managed to cling on to. I looked like Dobby the elf from Harry Potter! I was still not offered any pain relief but luckily my mum had some very strong pain-killers in her handbag, so I popped these like sweets. The staff saw we had our own pain relief and said, 'Do not take them.' So of course, we ignored them and I took more. They advised us they could not give me any pain relief until they knew what injury they were dealing with. I had never heard so much rubbish in my life. The first thing you do is get your patient stable and free from pain. Once more I found myself missing the NHS.

I was sent for an X ray and was shocked to experience yet again more very bad nursing care. I was dragged from the trolley on to the X-ray table, which was an inch lower than the trolley so I felt the bump as I landed. I was roughly handled and as I couldn't understand what they were saying or they me, I was using words not found in the English Dictionary. I was effing and jeffing and screaming, and the more I screamed the rougher they became.

I was then dragged back onto the trolley, this time over the lip of the X-ray table and by God the pain was excruciating.

'Ahhh! For fuck's sake!' I screamed (apologies for the

language but, by God, it was sore!) What was wrong with these people?

Back in the corridor and still without pain relief, I heard via my mum that I needed further X-rays. So, I had to endure all the same treatment all over again. This was supposed to be my holiday – to celebrate and relax after finishing chemo – and yet here I was back in hospital and unlucky enough to be on the same shift as shit nursing staff! Where were all the Florence Nightingales?

Jed finally found the hospital we were in after realising we weren't at the one he'd driven to. He managed to get hold of my mum on the phone and, luckily for him, we had been to the hospital with my mum just a few days earlier, so he knew where it was. Poor Jed drove in the dark, in a foreign country. How he managed to find his way is still a mystery to me.

So, my coccyx had a little fracture and the shock it had received had made it curl inwards on itself. No wonder I couldn't straighten up! They gave me an injection for the pain and sent me home in the ambulance – the same one I'd arrived in. Mum tipped the driver and his partner (like you do in a taxi), which I found strange. That said, Mum tips everyone so it shouldn't surprise me.

For the rest of the holiday I struggled to walk and had to take a cushion with me everywhere as I couldn't sit down properly. I had to sit on my side with the pillow wedged underneath me. I still struggle to this day with a sore coccyx and cannot sit for long periods. To top it all off my health card didn't work and I had to pay for the prescription for pain relief, which cost me sixty euros!

The Menopause

Part of my treatment following chemo was to be on Tamoxifen for ten years. This put me into a chemically-induced menopause, which comes with its own set of problems. I now have weight gain, hot flushes (which are horrible), sore joints, memory loss and my sleep pattern is just awful. It has been a horrendous time and, more than eight years on, I am still suffering from all of these symptoms – something else I've had to learn to live with. I was having two to three flushes every hour when it all first began, but now I only have them after eating or after having a hot drink and again throughout the night. I shouldn't grumble, at least I'm alive. But it's been such a long hard struggle, and just when I thought I was getting over one symptom, another one came along in its place.

According to Google there are actually thirty-four

symptoms of the menopause: hot flushes, night sweats, irregular periods, mood swings, vaginal dryness, decreased libido, headaches, breast soreness, burning mouth, joint pain, digestive problems, electric shocks, muscle tension, gum problems, tingling extremities, itchy skin, fatigue, anxiety, disrupted sleep, hair loss, memory lapses, difficulty in concentrating, weight gain, dizzy spells, bloating, stress incontinence, brittle nails, allergies, irregular heartbeat, body odour, irritability, depression, panic disorder, osteoporosis, wanting to kill your partner and a partridge in a pear tree!

You may not experience them all but from this list I have seventeen of them! Wow! I hadn't even known I had most of them. I had been so focused on my main ones – hot flushes, disturbed sleep, weight gain and vaginal dryness! Oh, and no, I don't have thoughts about killing Jed!

What us ladies have to put up with. This is why we are the superior sex. Can you imagine a man going through any of this? We would never hear the end of it. God help Jed when he gets a headache or back pain. I say, 'Ahh, does it hurt? Well take that pain and magnify it by 1000 and you get to experience a little of the pain I had when I had chemo.'

That soon shuts him up!

My menopause symptoms started one morning when I sat in front of my mirror applying makeup. I was looking well and then I saw it: a long blonde hair sprouting out of my chin. I was shocked. Where the hell did this come from? It was certainly not there yesterday when I put my make-up on. How can a hair grow so quickly?

Over the years these hairs have sprouted all over my face and I have to pluck on a daily basis and shave my moustache! Worst of all, I now get a hairy big toe! This is gross and nowhere in the books does it say that menopause will turn you into a man! And then along with the hairs came the flushes and within days I was a menopausal woman. Jed was lucky though as some women get very violent or moody when they hit the menopause but not me. I have remained as happy and chilled as I was before, and this will last as long as Jed doesn't get on my bloody nerves or drive me mad!

Tamoxifen has stopped me from producing oestrogen (one of the sex hormones) which means this part of my brain is now switched off (thank God, some would say). However, because my vagina is now deficient in oestrogen, it has started to dry up and become itchy. Good job the gynaecologist isn't attempting to shove anything up there now! It is paper-thin and, like all the other muscles in my body, lack of use has caused it to shrink and lose tone. This might make the men of us menopausal women think they've suddenly grown a larger penis, but I'm sorry to disappoint you boys, it's purely because our vaginas have shrunk! Furthermore, if I coughed or laughed, I wet myself. This was just great. The only good thing that came from having a hysterectomy was that it stopped me wetting myself. I could once again have a right good chuckle and the only thing that became damp was my eyes from crying with laughter.

'Chemo brain' was bad enough but the menopause brought its own memory loss and I find myself saying random words in place of what I should say: 'Get the washing out of the dishwasher', or 'Pass me the thingy – you know what I mean – you do. Stop being a pain, the thing with the buttons … yes that's what I meant: the remote. Jesus Jed! Stop being awkward you knew what I was trying to say!'

Most of the time I can't even retrieve the words to say what I want. Thankfully, Jed is so good as interpreting what I am trying to say. Then I do daft things like putting the milk in the cupboard and the cups in the fridge. But as I said, I've been very lucky not to suffer from mood swings so I am thankful for that … and I'm sure Jed is too.

One time I said to Jed, 'I'm going on the bike.' (I meant the running machine, which even now I call 'the bike'). Ten minutes later I found him in the garage with his helmet and biking gear on with our bikes all ready to go out.

'What are you doing?' I asked him.

'You said you wanted to go out on your bike.'

'No, I may have said bike, but I meant running machine. You should know what I mean for God's sake!'

He's not made that mistake again!

Menopause is not for the faint hearted and I feel for all those women going through it. I salute those that have passed through it and I feel sorry for those that have yet to experience it. My advice would be to laugh your way through it and don't be embarrassed to say when you are having a flush. Strip off when you need to, and always keep a fan and some water with you. Sleep naked and remember it won't last forever, even though it may feel like it. Like puberty, you will come out the other side! I saw a good post on the Internet that said, 'My memory is so bad that I could arrange a surprise party for myself and still surprise myself when it happened.' That tickled me. Yes, it really is that bad!

I have to continue taking Tamoxifen until I am about 53. It used to be that you only took it for five years, but they now have new research that shows cancer is less likely to return if you stay on this medication for ten years. After I stop taking it, I may go into a normal menopause. Let's hope not – ten years of menopause is quite enough, thank you! The thing with the menopause is, you don't realise you have hormones until they're gone. And it's only when you don't have them that you miss them. Because my cancer fed from my oestrogen, I am not allowed to have HRT. So, menopause is just something I have to deal with drug-free. It is a bit like giving birth naturally!

Unfortunately for me, two days after I turned fifty-one my flushes suddenly increased in intensity and I am now having a really bad menopause. My flushes are so bad I find myself naked most of the time around my house; I'm just so hot all the time. And now the flushes have increased in intensity, I'm wet through all the time. Just my luck!

Nodules

In December 2012 I had another scare. I saw my consultant as I was becoming breathless and he suggested I had a scan of my lungs to make sure the cancer had not come back and spread. They get me all the time; I wasn't expecting him to say that. This was a worrying time and the appointment we had for the results was just as bad.

We waited in anticipation in the waiting room of the hospital. We were going out after the appointment to do some Christmas shopping and we were excited to get the news that I was OK. The breathlessness would be nothing and we could go and celebrate. After a long wait (which is awful when you're waiting for results) the consultant said, 'We've looked at your scan and it appears to be OK.'

I realised Jed and I were holding our breaths as I heard a sharp exhale of relief come from both of us.

But then the consultant carried on speaking: 'But we did find a few nodules and we don't know exactly what they are. We will have to monitor them over the next nine months because nodules, if they are cancer, tend to grow very slowly on the lungs. So, we will rescan you in nine months' time, but don't worry.'

Don't worry? Are you having a laugh? You've just told me I may have a secondary cancer and you tell me not to worry. Jed and I were both in shock. This was not the news we were expecting and not the news we wanted. Needless to say, the next nine months were excruciating waiting for me to be rescanned, not knowing if the nodules were cancer and were slowly killing me. I was terrified and suddenly nine months felt like a very long time to have to wait.

We had many scans and examinations over the next year and a half and the first scan following the news that I had these nodules, revealed this: there were now three nodules in total. Two remained the same in size, one had disappeared, and one is 'slightly concerning'. Apparently, it was 'fluffy' in appearance and therefore suspicious. So, we had a suspicious-looking nodule and again we had to wait a further six months before I could be rescanned. Apparently, scanning me is just as damaging as the amount of radiation it produces can cause a lung cancer, so they make me wait.

The next time I am scanned and receive my results there is no change, so they don't think there is anything sinister going on. This was great news but still not the news I wanted – I wanted to hear that the nodules had all disappeared and there was nothing to worry about.

Since then I have lived with these nodules and

although I get breathless very easily, I'm sure it is not due to anything sinister.

It's always good to have friends and colleagues who work at the hospital and I managed to get my results from them as soon as they were available, instead of having to wait to see the consultant. On the occasion we went to the hospital to receive the results that revealed the 'fluffy' nodule, I had already received this news from one of my friends. I don't like sitting in the waiting room when I don't know the results; I get so anxious so I much prefer being told before the appointment.

When we got to the hospital the consultant said the results weren't back. Ha! Liar! We knew they were back as we'd already been told them. I couldn't tell the doctor this though as it would reveal I'd already seen them. I asked him to look again and said I'd been told they were back, which was why I'd been given the appointment to come in. He had another look and apologised saying yes, they were actually back, but the radiologist has not reported on them and he was not qualified to interpret them. Then he sent us away and told us to come back another day. What a great service!

On one occasion we were due to go for a scan which would tell the consultant what the nodules had been doing over the last few months. I had waited for nearly nine months for this scan but when we woke up on the morning of the scan, we were shocked to see it had snowed very heavily overnight. Now normally I would love this, but I'd waited nine months for this scan; nothing was going to stop me getting to the hospital to have it carried out! However, this was no normal snow fall, this was a blizzard. We managed to get into my dad's car, but the snow was so heavy that the roads were impassable. Cars had been abandoned on the road and there were long queues of traffic all stuck in the snow. We were going nowhere. The wind screen was covered and the wipers couldn't keep up with the speed of the snow fall. My dad couldn't see anything in front of him. It was absolute carnage and a complete whiteout. He said, 'You have no chance of getting to the hospital.' We had been in the car for almost an hour and had not managed to move anywhere. My appointment time was looming, and I was in full panic mode. This was just awful! But no way was I going to miss the scan.

So, I said, 'I'll walk'. I jumped out of the car and began the tedious task of walking to the hospital. My poor mum jumped out with me. I tried to make her stay in the car but she was adamant she was coming with me. Now the hospital is over an hour's walk from where we live so this was not going to be an easy task but as you know by now, I am stubborn and determined. So, unprepared for a walk in the snow, without enough warm clothes, we set off.

We had to keep our heads down as, unfortunately for us, the wind was blowing the snow straight into us as we walked. We were getting its full force in our faces. The snow was thick and every step was an effort. Luckily, because it was so deep on the pavement, it wasn't slippy. The flurry of fresh snow erased our footprints as we walked so no one could have followed our tracks even if they'd wanted to. The whirling wind whipped up the snow, covering us from head to toe and slowing us down. I ignored the pain from the piercing wind, which went straight through my boob and back, and pushed on through the storm. Mum was right behind me, frozen stiff but determined to stay and support me. I should have turned around and gone home for the sake of my poor mum, but my determination to get to the hospital was so strong I couldn't give up.

The route to the hospital was mostly up hill, so this was a really difficult trek. I felt like I was practising to scale Everest. This would be the closest I would get to ever experiencing weather like you get in the Himalayas. Maybe this was a slight exaggeration, but you know what I mean. Then a lorry drove past and soaked us with slushy wet snow from the side of the road all over us. We'd now been walking for over an hour and a half and we were nearly there. I phoned my friend who lived by the hospital and asked if she could meet us and drive us the last part. Thankfully she did and when we finally arrived at the hospital, we were frozen, wet through and tired. But we had done it. Poor Mum, her legs were red raw and sore as she only had thin leggings on – we'd not been anticipating this walk and weren't prepared.

When we got to the scan department, the nurse said, 'Oh we weren't expecting anyone. We didn't think anyone would come in this weather and were about to close.'

"NOOO! You can't close – I have just battled the storm for over an hour and a half to get here for this scan!'

She looked at me and then at my mum, both of us cold, wet and tired and said, 'Are you mad?'

I got my scan and then Mum and I looked at each other and realisation hit us both. I said, 'What now? How do we get home?'

***

Eight years after this journey started, I discovered a small patch of dry skin on my right shoulder (the same side I'd had breast cancer). The GP had a look at it and said it didn't look suspicious, but due to my previous diagnosis they would refer me to the skin clinic to be on the safe side.

The consultant I saw at the skin clinic was under the same impression. She wasn't concerned but said she would do a biopsy just to be sure. I was really worried about having yet another biopsy, especially when none of the doctors thought it was anything suspicious. I didn't want to put my body through any more stress if it was avoidable. But we had been here before – being told it was nothing suspicious, so I couldn't take any chances; I would have to have the biopsy.

It was a different consultant who carried out the biopsy and he too confirmed I had nothing to worry about. He said, 'We'll do the biopsy but I've seen many skin cancers and this doesn't look like a typical skin cancer.'

What a relief.

One week later the results were back and hey, guess what: it tested positive for skin cancer. A single-cell melanoma. I had to have it removed, which was another scary moment for me. The surgeon was very good though. She was very gentle with me. She knew I was vulnerable when it came to cancer and surgery and she did all she could to make me feel at ease. She told me it would take twenty minutes to remove and I was to have a local anaesthetic.

As they were numbing the area, she asked the assisting nurse for more of the anaesthetic; she was going to remove a little more skin than she first thought, but the nurse said, 'We don't have any more.'

What she should have said was that they had no more anaesthetic on the trolley but that she would go and get some. The surgeon said, 'Don't say that in front of Carolann and scare her like that. We have plenty of anaesthetic – don't worry, Carolann.'

Thank God for that! As she cauterised the wound you could smell the burnt flesh, so I concentrated on the clock as she carried out the procedure, waiting for it all to be over. And exactly twenty minutes later it was done.

Once the procedure was finished, I was put in another cubicle to wait for an aftercare nurse to discuss what would happen next. As soon as she walked in, she said, 'They've just cauterised your skin, haven't they? I can smell the burning flesh – it's such a distinctive smell!'

The scar healed as a keloid scar, which was really itchy and inflamed, and it drove me mad for the first few months. They treated it with steroid tape, which helped flatten the scar and remove the itch. Now I have to stay out of the sun, use factor 50 sun cream and wear cotton clothes, large sun hats and sunglasses to keep me fully covered up.

The End of the Ride

This had been the biggest and scariest rollercoaster ride I had ever been on. I've been up and down more times than a yoyo! I've been through the mill, as they say. I have had every scan I think they can offer; I've had needles, cannulas, dyes put through me (which, for a few seconds, make you think you've wet yourself); I've had to drink liquids and potions which make my body glow; I've also had my share of radiation (at one point they gave me a letter because I was going to Spain and the radiation may show up going through security – luckily, it didn't). I've had mammograms, been sliced open, had parts removed, parts replaced, had drains, drips, injections, medication (*loads* of medication), had a catheter, been poisoned, been depressed, laughed, cried, nearly died (or felt like I was dying), been poisoned five further times, sent into a menopause, had hot flushes, experienced weight gain and a dried up vagina (that's a bad one), had pain, *so much pain*, sickness, exhaustion, lost my hair, been up and down and round and round … the list goes on and on. But I'm still here, as strong as ever and determined to keep as fit and healthy as I can.

I had been on a terrifying ride and I never ever want to repeat it. But my story proves that regardless of what life throws at you, you can survive. I am one of the lucky ones who have survived cancer, got through chemo and all the treatment associated with this nasty disease, which doesn't discriminate, regardless of age, gender, or race. If you are experiencing or ever have to experience any of what I've gone through, you will get through it all no matter how bad it seems at the time. My ride has now come to end. It has flattened every ounce of my strength and energy, punished me in every sadistic way possible and taken me to some of the darkest, scariest places of my entire life. I have been to hell and back, but I am Carolann Bruce and nothing keeps me down for long. I have bounced back even stronger, more positive and determined to live and enjoy every moment of my life.

I have been there, done it and I was NOT doing it again. Or was I?

Today I am sitting in the car park of the private hospital, where I had my first appointment, my scans and biopsy. It is raining as I write this.

My beautiful daughter has found a lump in her breast. I have felt it and it's quite large, but I am sure it is a cyst. My gut instinct tells me it is nothing to worry about. I pray to God that it's nothing more sinister and I am not wrong. We are in the time of coronavirus and therefore some places are still closed. Those that are open, like the hospital, will only allow the patient in and not any relatives. Initially we had to have a video call with her GP because she was not allowed to go to into the practice. Following she call she was offered an appointment to see a GP later that afternoon. We had to sit in the car outside the surgery until they phoned and told her she could come in. I was not allowed to go with her so I remained in the car.

She was only in the surgery for five minutes and came back saying the doctor had said he would refer her and this could take up to two weeks. No way could I wait that long for an appointment so, once again, I phoned the private hospital and booked her in for the very next day. Luckily the next day was Tuesday and, as we all know, Tuesday is the one-stop breast clinic day, so I was sure she'd be seen by a consultant and be able to have all the tests that she needed. I told the receptionist that my consultant hadn't turned up when I had booked in and we needed to make sure this consultant was definitely going to be there. She said she would email him directly, let him know we were coming and book Jenna in for a scan.

As coincidences go, she got my consultant – the second one I'd had, not the one who carried out my surgery. And this other consultant was very nice; she would be in safe hands with him. I managed to get as much information as possible regarding the costs but the receptionist on the phone didn't have the exact costs she said, which is ridiculous. Everything she quoted was 'approximately' this and 'approximately' that. She said:

9.30am to see the consultant approx. £250

10am to have a scan approx. £350

10.30am to see the consultant again approx. £150

So here we are, outside the private hospital again, in the same carpark I made the phone call to Kimberley the evening I was diagnosed. I've not been back to this hospital in more than eight years and being here waiting for my beautiful daughter in these circumstances is heartbreaking. What's worse, due to COVID-19, I'm not allowed to accompany her, so she is in the hospital with a lump in her breast having to go through these tests on her own.

I know this is going to be OK because my gut says it is, but that does not stop me from worrying. I have asked her to keep sending me updates so I know what's happening. I am writing this chapter as I sit in the car waiting for her.

Then my phone beeps and I see Jenna's first message come through:

I am going in now.

OMG! My heart is beating so fast I feel sick. Five minutes later the phone beeps again. This time it says:

He thinks it is just a cyst, but he sending me for a scan to be sure. He said it is the size of a pea.

I am so relieved and once again my gut instinct was right. I phone my mum and as soon as I heard her beautiful voice on the other end of the line I start to cry. This was all so real again; I was reliving it all, sitting in this car park with all my memories and being so worried about my daughter.

Once more, my phone beeps and it's Jenna:

The scan has confirmed it is a cyst and as long as it does not get any larger than a fivepence piece they will not need to do anything. It is in the same breast as you had yours and not far off being in the same area.

When Jenna came back to the car, she hugged me and I cried, I was so relieved to have good news. We had been lucky today and had dodged another bullet. We have her NHS appointment in two weeks' times, which we will still go to as planned; a second opinion can save lives. And if the cyst continues to grow, then in two weeks we will have an update. I would rather be safe than sorry. My experience has taught me to always trust your gut instinct, always get things checked out, and always seek a second opinion if you are unhappy or unsure. *Know your body*. Never just trust the opinion of your GP or consultant. My story proves that sometimes they do get it wrong.

I thank the Universe every day for giving me a second chance. I am the richest person in the world as I have my health. Without good health you have nothing.

Thank you, Universe, for my perfect health. My perfect health keeps me alive.